HOW TO
write
WELL

**WHEN YOU DON'T
KNOW WHERE
TO START**

SUSAN FEEHAN

How to Write Well

First published in 2015 by

Panoma Press
48 St Vincent Drive, St Albans,
Herts, AL1 5SJ, UK
info@panomapress.com
www.panomapress.com

Book layout by Neil Coe

Printed on acid-free paper from managed forests.

ISBN 978-1-909623-77-4

To my family, friends and colleagues
who helped me to get here with advice,
encouragement and the occasional glass of
champagne. You know who you are.

TESTIMONIALS

'A stunning array of writing tips, humour and stories makes this an essential and highly valuable book for those who need to write well'

MINDY GIBBINS-KLEIN, FOUNDER OF THE BOOK MIDWIFE®

'Invaluable. So many great writing tips in such a small book'

ANN MARTIN, PUBLIC SERVICE WORKER

'Great writing tips and insights, delivered at a fast pace. Proof that less is more'

HELEN TIFFANY, COACH AND TRAINING COMPANY OWNER

'A no-nonsense guide, essential for writers — which means everyone'

**STEPHEN RAYNER,
FREELANCE SUB-EDITOR**

'A refreshing new approach packed with practical hot tips to help dodge common pitfalls'

**JEFF DAVY,
FREELANCE JOURNALIST AND
UNIVERSITY LECTURER**

'I love it. It puts passion into the technical business of good writing'

**KEITH MCDONALD,
RETIRED JOURNALIST**

'If I had to give young writers advice, I'd say don't listen to writers talking about writing.'

LILLIAN HELLMAN

INTRODUCTION

MY mother told me I flirted briefly as a child — for a fortnight, in fact — with the idea of becoming a 'ballerina on ice' when I grew up. I'm pleased to say that idea fizzled away and I returned to my first love: writing.

Journalism was the obvious way of getting paid to write, partly because I had no idea how to become a novelist or screenwriter. Mind you, I wasn't convinced that I'd be able to hold down a writing job on a newspaper or magazine.

I fixated on the thought that I'd be writing about fires and natural disasters but there was a problem: I couldn't drive. I imagined arriving on the 155 bus far too late, when disaster had been overcome and there was no one around to tell me their stories. There would be no one to ask, 'How do you feel?' as I gazed at the toasted ruins of someone's beloved home.

I was seven, with sleepless nights about an uncertain future.

Eventually, it dawned on me that I could learn to drive when I was older. Sleep and happy thoughts returned. What joy! I would be on the spot when people were going through the wringer.

In the years to come, I became a journalist but never really wrote about natural disasters, aside from one fairly impressive fire and two murders. Instead, I wrote about DIY, business leaders and how they ran their empires, and finance — a subject I never imagined, as a child, I'd find every bit as drama-packed and fascinating as fires.

I met business leaders with pin-sharp instincts on how to build a great company or rescue a failing one. Yet few had any idea how to write, or a clue about where and how to start. Where writing was concerned, sensible judgment often deserted them. So they employed someone to do it for them, not necessarily with fabulous results.

I moved into sub-editing and also trained journalists for leading magazine publishers, meeting reporters who had similar writing issues to people in business. Some couldn't recognise a great story if it smacked them round the face with a cold, wet flannel. But they could assemble a coherent, grammatically pure sentence about nothing worth reading. Others, often experts in a niche area, could entice a front-page lead from a sedimentary rock but couldn't make it sing as a piece of writing. A handful could do both with equal skill. They often became sub-editors, a group once described by the columnist Miles Kington as 'the diamond cutters of journalism'. If you want to obsess over a particular subject for the whole of your career, you become a reporter; if you want to obsess over words and writing, you become a sub.

Years of reading and editing other people's work taught me that writing either oozes a charm that seduces and holds you captive or it gives off a stink that makes you gag. Writing has a subtle quality that muscles its way into the work, sitting quietly between the lines. Gravitas. Uncertainty. Soul. Confusion. Depending on the knowledge and confidence of the writer, an intangible quality shines through.

And that discovery drove me to write this book.

No, not true. Not yet.

As a sub-editor, I looked at separate stories in a newspaper and realised they would be more interesting if you cobbled them together as the starting point for a decent film story. Since this wasn't a skill newspaper and magazine publishers approved of, I wrote a screenplay, a move I blame on my father. He had worked in the film industry and force-fed me the classics; I still recall minutiae about black-and-white films that no child ought to be able to recall when they've forgotten the name of their best friend at school. My mother and I almost set up home at our local library, so I might have written a novel, were it not for laziness and ignorance.

Novels are longer than screenplays, many of which barely reach 25,000 words, the character names gobbling up about a quarter of that total. A screenplay seemed easier, something to be dashed off quickly, much longer than a magazine feature, but still manageable.

Rookie mistake.

Several screenplays later, it paid off. Or so I thought.

People became excited about a romantic comedy I had written. Let's do lunch, producers would say. Sign this deal, they said. We can't pay any money upfront, but stick with us and we'll make you rich, they promised. It'll be fun, they said...

Well, they didn't make me rich — not yet, at least — and it was as frustrating as much as it was fun. Indie film producers with assorted, but usually thin, experience struggled to raise money in a country where the film industry often feels more like a lifestyle choice than it does a fully-fledged industry.

One producing team raised $15 million to make the film, but from an investor who wasn't really keen on films. He was a 'suit'. So the money came and went, as that kind of money does, finding its way into a lower- risk industry — mobile phones in China, probably.

It was frustrating, particularly for someone used to an industry where people make quick decisions, act on them and produce fast results. Bish, bash, bosh, and there's a fresh edition of a newspaper pleading to be read. The film industry is the polar opposite, with people always talking about doing something next month or next year, sometimes even the year after next or the one after that. And these distant, future plans are often delayed.

This frustration led me to make a classic wrong step — or not, depending on how you see it. I was surrounded by the core of a useful production team and, incurable research junkie that I am, I'd soaked up enough about film financing to be able to have a sensible discussion. The team suggested that we raise the money ourselves — meaning me.

The financial phenomenon we call crowdfunding caught my attention. The crowd would help us to get the film financed. A pitch wouldn't raise the entire budget, but we'd be nearer to our goal. It would be fun.

I tested our pitch on a crowdfund guru and a film accountant. They thought it was fabulous, utter genius. It was a slam-dunk success, people said... until it wasn't.

Within 24 hours of launching our £140,000 campaign, it was clear we were going to crash and burn and it was going to be ugly. The middle of a pitch is when you discover that crowdfunding is a blood sport — you have everything on the line and can only hear the silence of everyone saying 'we don't get it'.

During the dark days of the pitch, some 100-year-old words lifted me each day, words that formed part of a speech delivered by Theodore Roosevelt, 26th President of the United States, at the Sorbonne in Paris: words that have become famous as 'the man in the arena' speech.

'It is not the critic who counts; not the man who points out how the strong man stumbles, or where the doer of deeds could have done them better.

'The credit belongs to the man who is actually in the arena, whose face is marred by dust and sweat and blood, who strives valiantly; who errs, who comes short again and again, because there is no effort without error and shortcoming; but who does actually strive to do the deeds; who knows great enthusiasms, the great devotions; who spends himself in a worthy cause; who at the best knows in the end the triumph of high achievement, and who at the worst, if he fails, at least fails while daring greatly, so that his place shall never be with those cold and timid souls who neither know victory nor defeat.'

If these words fail to move you, I suggest you return your soul for a good scrubbing and MOT. When all seems lost, these are the kind of words that remind us why all is not lost at all.

Did these words raise our funding? No. Our campaign was flawed and our target too high, all of which is a subject for a different book.

The true campaign reward became clear. It lay in the power of well-crafted words to motivate, to drive someone to carry on through exhaustion and despair. The power of words to change us and the world we live in.

In the aftermath of our exhausting crowdfund, I stood back, allowing others to take up the fundraising reins while I returned to what I do best — writing, and helping people to write well.

We put our thoughts, knowledge and ideas into what we write. We fill it with our passions, sometimes creating new businesses, new jobs, new organisations that work to make the world better than the one we already have.

We write to discover and share what we think, what we feel, and what we know.

We write to discover gems of ideas that nudge the world a little. Sometimes we start seismic revolutions, using words to form nations or write laws that embody our principles. We hold people to account and we inspire them. We connect.

Maybe you want to build a world-class brand, a company that crashes into the Fortune 500, or create a career that leaves a lasting impact on the planet.

Whatever you want to achieve, writing is your best buddy, the go-to sidekick who can help you get to where you want to go. It's personal. Not just in novels, poetry, and screenplays, or inspirational speeches; even in business, writing is personal. In emails, and business plans and strategy documents, in mission statements and social media posts, you are what you write.

And yet... you have a distinct unease about where to start, what to say and how to say it.

And if you are what you write, why can't you do it well?

That's why I wrote this book.

'The scariest moment is just before you start.'

STEPHEN KING

HOW TO USE THIS BOOK

MY aim with this book is to offer a holistic approach to writing. It means avoiding blueprints and templates, or concentrating purely on hard-and-fast grammar and punctuation rules. Tips and guidelines are fine, and you'll find lots of them here. Grammar, punctuation and spelling are important — as long as we accept that powerful writing often breaks rules.

Craft skills of language have a vital place in helping you to produce strong, clear writing, but they won't prop you up if you don't know where to start. Neither do blueprints and templates help when you don't have much to say.

So the primary aim of this book is to show you writing as a process, offering you a touchstone to keep you on course as you write. I want you to discover why you write and what your writing says about you, show you how it can help to expand your world, and how to diagnose and fix your writing troubles when they haunt you.

I'll offer guidance and suggestions at each stage, but deciding what to take on board is *your* choice. What you write reflects who you are; the last thing you need is someone making decisions for you. What you need are options about how to connect to the rest of the world in a way that makes an accurate and confident statement about who you are and what you want to achieve.

With this in mind, I'd suggest reading the book from start to finish. I'm taking a step-by-step approach and the book makes more sense if you read about these in the right order. I know some readers will flip to chapters where they already know they need to focus. There is nothing wrong with that as long as you soak up the process too.

No one has all the answers where good writing is concerned. What we can discover are tactics that suit us as individuals and for what we want our writing to achieve.

If this book helps you to get some writing clarity — and I sincerely hope it does — my work will be done.

'If you want to change the world, pick up your pen and write.'

MARTIN LUTHER

CONTENTS – SHOW ME THE LIST

PART ONE

Who we are, why we write...
and what stops us from
doing it well.

'There is a door we all want to go through and writing can help you find it and open it.'

ANNE LAMOTT

'It's not the fear of writing that blocks people. It's the fear of not writing well, something quite different.'

SCOTT BERKUN

'I have spent a good many years – too many, I think – being ashamed of what I write.'

STEPHEN KING

'In order to write the book you want to write, in the end you have to become the person you need to become to write that book.'

JUNOT DÍAZ

CHAPTER ONE

Writing badly – a crime novel, or just a crime?

AN anonymous tip leads journalists to team up with forensic experts and uncover a mystery about a household name. This sounds like a teaser for a whodunit — but it's more of a who-wrote-it.

A story without bullets, knives, corpses or stolen jewels. Instead, a story about words, personal tics of language usage, forensic linguistics experts and a newsworthy literary confession. While it starts with a Twitter tip, it ends with the revelation that JK Rowling wrote a crime novel under a pseudonym.

The story of how journalists uncovered the Harry Potter author's secret made headlines of its own. And the way *The Sunday Times* built its case offers evidence that *we are what we write*.

It began with a tweet from a member of staff at *The Sunday Times*, praising newly published crime novel *The Cuckoo's Calling* and remarking that it didn't feel like the work of a debut author. The novice writer was Robert Galbraith, whose biography described him as an ex-military police investigator who'd left the army to work in private security.

An anonymous reply to the tweet claimed that *Calling* was not a debut novel at all, but the work of Harry Potter creator JK Rowling. When the newspaper pressed for detail, the Twitter account was closed and the whistleblower disappeared.

Minor detective work uncovered the fact that *The Cuckoo's Calling* shared the same agent, publisher and editor as Rowling's previous non-Harry Potter book *The Casual Vacancy*. The tip's credibility grew.

Sunday Times arts editor Richard Brooks read *The Cuckoo's Calling* and grew sceptical about the writing squaring with Galbraith's military background. Brooks called in two forensic linguistics experts to help solve the mystery.

Peter Millican, lecturer in philosophy and computing at Oxford University, and Patrick Juola, a computer science professor at Duquesne University in Pittsburgh agreed to conduct separate linguistics analyses. Each man had eight texts to analyse: Galbraith's novel *The Cuckoo's Calling*, Rowling's post-Harry Potter book *The Casual Vacancy*, and two novels apiece from three other British crime authors — Ruth Rendell, PD James and Val McDermid.

Juola ran the texts through JGAAP — short for Java Graphical Authorship Attribution Program — a computer program he'd been developing with the help of students for more than ten years. He chose four separate groups of writing features for analysis:

- The distribution of word lengths. What percentage of a book is made up of words of a certain length? What's the frequency between each of them? This test gave Juola one of the strongest clues that Rowling was Galbraith.

- The 100 most commonly used words — even ones as basic as 'the' and 'of' leave a hidden signature.

- The distribution of character 4-grams — groups of four adjacent characters, sometimes as words, parts of words or even parts of two words.

- The frequency of word pairings, a feature that shows not just what you're talking about but how you refer to it and what you describe in the same way.

It took Juola 90 minutes to crunch the results, and the approach may seem bizarre to those of us who aren't experts in forensic linguistics. Even Juola is clear that this kind of judgment is not cut-and-dried, offering indications about authorship rather than a bankable verdict.

But when compared with Galbraith, all the authors — other than Rowling — were ruled out by at least one of Juola's tests. His analysis showed that only one writer in 16 was likely to have a style similar to Galbraith's. Rowling was one of them.

In the UK, Millican conducted his own analysis and asked for extra texts from each of the famous authors, using *Harry Potter and the Deathly Hallows* as the second Rowling book.

All the books went through Signature — Millican's linguistics software. It has a method that compares authorship on six features: word length, sentence length, paragraph length, letter frequency, punctuation frequency, and word usage.

A few potentially distinctive words cropped up, so Millican turned to the 500 most common words in each book as extra clues, removing words likely to skew the results — words such as 'Harry', 'wand' and 'police'.

Word usage emerged as Millican's most compelling reason to support the Rowling-as-Galbraith tip, with *The Cuckoo's Calling* closest to Rowling's style than any other of the samples. Millican's verdict took five hours to produce.

With both investigations indicating that Rowling was Galbraith — it was time for *The Sunday Times* to call the Harry Potter author.

Had she written the Galbraith novel? When Rowling confessed, the newspaper had a story that set the literary world abuzz.

After being outed, Rowling said: 'I hoped to keep this secret a little longer, because being Robert Galbraith has been such a liberating experience! It has been wonderful to publish without hype or expectation and pure pleasure to get feedback from publishers and readers under a different name.'

The revelation included a bonus. When Rowling's secret became public, *The Cuckoo's Calling* shot from 4,709th on Amazon's list to number one. Sales of the book rose by more than 500,000 per cent.

JK Rowling is by no means the first author to write under a pseudonym. Murder mystery novelist Agatha Christie wrote romance novels as Mary Westmacott. Stephen King, Isaac Asimov, CS Lewis, Michael Crichton, Ruth Rendell... these are just a handful of authors who have disguised their writing identities for a mix of personal and professional reasons.

Of course, some people have criminal reasons for wanting their authorship to remain a mystery. We should be grateful that forensic linguistics plays an increasing role in foiling their plans.

In 1995, writing style helped to capture the man who had terrorised the United States with a series of explosions that earned him the name Unabomber. In an attempt to stop the attacks, *The New York Times* and *The Washington Post* agreed to publish a 35,000-word manifesto setting out the Unabomber's aims.

David Kaczynski saw it and was struck by a particular phrase used, — 'you can't eat your cake and have it, too' — instead of the more common 'you can't have your cake and eat it, too'. The unusual version was used by his brother Ted — a gifted academic who attended Harvard at 16 and went on to become a mathematician and self-taught survivalist. The 'cake' phrase was strong enough to prompt David to call the FBI about the possibility of his brother being the Unabomber, and Ted Kaczynski's 17- year bombing campaign — which had killed three people and injured 23 — was brought to an end.

You might imagine that pinning down authorship with certainty calls for analysis of thousands of words. But you'd be wrong.

Text messages helped to bring about the downfall of wealthy businessman Howard Simmerson, who was convicted of murdering Julie Turner, a woman living in Yorkshire, when she disappeared in 2005. The couple had met through a lonely hearts column, and Simmerson had lavished £200,000 in gifts on Turner during the next four years. In fact, she was wearing a diamond-studded gold watch when Simmerson stuffed her body into an oil drum.

During his trial, evidence showed that Simmerson's writing style shared features with text messages supposed to be from Turner. Simmerson is serving a minimum 25- year sentence.

It's hard to believe a short writing sample can generate reliable analysis. Yet it can. Christopher Coleman was convicted of the 2009 murder of his family in Illinois partly on the grounds that his writing style matched spray-painted threats at the family home.

Writing style can even save an author's life. A man faced certain deportation from the US, until linguistics analysis showed him to be the author of anonymous newspaper articles criticising the government of his native country. Authorities granted him leave to stay in the US and he avoided the hostile reception waiting for him at home.

These stories share a common thread: the use of forensic linguistics as identifying tools, an approach mostly carried out for legal reasons. Is a suicide note a cover for a murder? Is a confession genuine or one fabricated by police? Is a ransom note from an outsider or is a kidnapping an inside job? Or, can linguistics support a fascinating story about a crime novel being written by a bestselling author who would prefer to remain anonymous?

If you've come through university in the digital age, you'll be familiar with the use of software to detect work plagiarised by students and presented as original. But you may be unaware that Wikipedia has developed an algorithm to safeguard the credibility of its website by unmasking 'sock puppet' accounts, set up by users who are paid by companies to edit Wikipedia's content in their favour.

Wikipedia examined 600 of its staff-led sock puppet investigations and developed an algorithm that scans 230 features of the writing, including grammatical quirks. Results showed the algorithm could predict which accounts were puppets with a 75 per cent accuracy rate.

Sophisticated programs can reveal identity in a different way: they uncover clues about our lifestyles purely from our posts on social media and through product reviews on sites such as Amazon.

The analysis is about more than exposing phoney praise. The way we write helps researchers to tailor marketing tactics with the demographic information buried in our feedback. Phrases used only in particular regions help companies to discover where their products are loved or hated, and they take action on the basis of these results.

The US Secret Service is even looking for a Twitter sarcasm detector to form part of a software system that examines social media posts. The aim is to filter people who want to rant in public from those who pose a public threat.

Yet Twitter reveals far more than sarcasm. Website analyzewords.com ranks 11 personality traits of Twitter users, based on the most recent 1,000 words in their history. Simply type your Twitter handle onto the website, or the handle of someone you want to assess, and you'll discover a breakdown of emotional, social, and thinking styles. Irresistible.

I emerged as equally upbeat as the Dalai Lama on 99; we were both beaten by the Pope who has an upbeat rating of 100. The Dalai Lama is angrier yet also more personable than me, but I'm more worried. I doubt that I'm ready for his job.

According to the website, US President Barack Obama and UK Prime Minister David Cameron are both angry. Obama is also arrogant and distant, while Cameron is depressed and worried. Business leaders Richard Branson and Lord Sugar are both arrogant, but Branson is upbeat while Sugar is depressed. Actor Tom Hanks is surprisingly worried, while UK writer, actor and broadcaster Stephen Fry is upbeat with a sensory thinking style.

We choose our words carefully, at least that's what we try to do, but we're giving away hidden personal information without realising it.

Along with other language obsessives, I'd like to think that one day I'll read a news story about a murderer being locked up because he can't spell... but it's more complex than that.

Where writing well is our concern, these stories may seem like red herrings borrowed from a novel. But they make the point that we cannot escape showing who we are.

What we write and how we express it gives away as much information as our dress sense, body language and interior design choices. It may make us uneasy, but we lay out our personalities, our quirks and our underlying beliefs with each word we write.

Change your writing and you change yourself.

'No two writers have the same set of creative fingerprints.'

LAUREN SAPALA

'We are all apprentices in a craft where no one ever becomes a master.'

ERNEST HEMINGWAY

CHAPTER TWO

You are what you write

THE idea of a personal writing fingerprint is not as far-fetched as it seems. Daily we make judgments, based on what we read, about the personality, credibility and trustworthiness of people we've never met or spoken to.

Don't think you're that judgmental? Read the following paragraphs and jot down three words that describe the writer.

> *'If you think an apostrophe was one of the 12 disciples of Jesus, you will never work for me. If you think a semicolon is a regular colon with an identity crisis, I will not hire you. If you scatter commas into a sentence with all the discrimination of a shotgun, you might make it to the foyer before we politely escort you from the building.*
>
> *'Some might call my approach to grammar extreme, but I prefer Lynne Truss's more cuddly phraseology: I am a grammar*

"stickler." And, like Truss — author of Eats, Shoots & Leaves — I have a "zero tolerance approach" to grammar mistakes that make people look stupid.

'Now, Truss and I disagree on what it means to have "zero tolerance." She thinks that people who mix up their itses "deserve to be struck by lightning, hacked up on the spot and buried in an unmarked grave," while I just think they deserve to be passed over for a job — even if they are otherwise qualified for the position.'

The words I'd choose are these: direct, decisive, opinionated.

The extract is from a blog by Kyle Wiens, chief executive of iFixit.com, the world's largest online repair manual. He also runs Dozuki, which helps companies write their own technical documents, such as paperless work instructions and step-by-step user manuals.

Grammar testing is compulsory for anyone who applies for a job with Wiens. Those who fail are shown the door. Wiens believes people who make fewer grammar mistakes make fewer mistakes when doing something unrelated to writing, even stocking shelves or labelling parts.

You may think his approach is too broad — although I don't. But that's not the point. You didn't have a problem choosing three adjectives, did you?

> ## HORROR STORY #1 – THE MANUAL ROAD TO BANKRUPTCY
>
> A computer manufacturer lost $35m in a single quarter in 1983 and eventually went out of business. Why? Customers bought a new line of the company's computers, and then rushed to return them because they found the instruction manuals to be badly written to the point of being incomprehensible.

WHO AM I? MORE IMPORTANTLY, WHO ARE YOU?

By now, you have a reasonably clear idea of who I am, based on what you've read so far — a mix of my content and the way I've expressed it. There's also a chance you have little idea of how your own writing comes across to your readers.

When you speak, you may be clear, to the point, and use short words in coherent sentences. When writing, you may be the opposite. You may throw in quasi-legal language you are ill-equipped to use when you write to a solicitor. You may throw in financial jargon in an email to your accountant, while having little idea what it means. Writing can do that to people.

You don't need a linguistics expert who can analyse your writing. For our purposes, the issue is essence of authorship more than ownership. We want to see what your writing says about you.

THE SUBJECTIVE, TOUCHY-FEELY APPROACH

Discover who you are as a writer by giving a motley mix of people something you've written, and asking for a three-adjective reaction.

People may want to elaborate or justify their comments. **STOP THEM**. You want three words only. When people overthink their choices, they spoil your chance of an authentic result.

Be prepared to interpret their reactions. You're being given clues about your writing; it's up to you to work out what these clues mean. Your instincts will show you the difference between accurate comments and misguided attempts to flatter.

You will get comments you love, and others you hate. Some may make your blood boil. These comments are the most valuable.

Having the urge to punch someone because they describe your writing as *pompous, long-winded,* or *tedious* is a slam-dunk sign that they're right. That's why it hurts. It's the thing you hate most about your writing, something you want to hide more than anything else.

Treat these violent urges as a gift, a sign about where to focus your attention. The pain will pass.

Avoid looking for praise, but accept it when it feels genuine. Warning: some comments may appear kind, while hiding criticism. If someone describes your writing as *direct*, ask yourself if this is a compliment about ideas expressed in well-structured sentences and presented in a coherent order without wasting a word, or does *direct* mean *angry* or *rude*?

Is *clear* a euphemism for *simplistic*? Does *ambitious* mean *deluded*? Does *inspirational* imply *grandiose*? Is *long* a kind way to say *boring*? *Effective* and *informative* may mean *dull*. Does *professional* suggest *predictable*?

You can take feedback at face value, or you may be able to read further into it. Don't try to overcook comments; just ask yourself what you were trying to achieve with your writing.

Did you play it safe? Were you bored, wishing that a report you needed to finish would disappear? Were you trying to impress your boss or a client? Did you put on a show, hoping people would be dazzled by your use of jargon? Did you write for yourself or for your readers?

Emotional reactions to your writing are comments about more than language skills. They are a snapshot of how you think, what you know, and what you feel. Strengths. Weaknesses. Knowledge. Passion. Boredom. Everything's there with nowhere to hide.

Maybe some objective analysis will be kind...

THE OBJECTIVE, ANAL-RETENTIVE APPROACH

Software analysis is the comfort zone of writing feedback. It makes you lazy — but you go there anyway. Few of us have access to the software used to analyse JK Rowling's style, but we know how to spellcheck our work — sometimes with clumsy results.

A Google search will throw up good and bad reviews of any writing analysis software; it is best approached with scepticism and used as an analytic tool, rather than as quality control. Software won't tell you if your work is capable of winning a Nobel Prize for literature, and it will find fault with work that does win. You will never win an A+ verdict from software, so don't try. And you may get that deflating back-at-school feeling, the one that says you're being marked.

Language software will sometimes suggest changes that would kill your writing, and it will want to add mistakes to work that's pretty damned powerful. Only a fool takes software comments as... foolproof.

So why are we bothering with it? Because you'll do it anyway in a moment of weakness. You may as well explore it under supervision. And software may show you some habits you don't realise you have.

Blunt is the word to remember. You have been warned...

First, let's generate our verdict of writing we're going to run through three forms of software analysis.

> *Here's to the crazy ones. The misfits. The rebels. The troublemakers. The round pegs in the square holes. The ones who see things differently. They're not fond of rules. And they have no respect for the status quo. You can quote them, disagree with them, glorify or vilify them. About the only thing*

you can't do is ignore them. Because they change things. They push the human race forward. And while some may see them as the crazy ones, we see genius. Because the people who are crazy enough to think they can change the world, are the ones who do.

These words formed part of Apple's 'Think Different' ad campaign, which was initiated by Steve Jobs in the late 1990s on his return to save the struggling company he'd co-founded years before. The campaign featured two ads, each using these words in a voiceover by actor Richard Dreyfus.

One version showed these words appearing on-screen gradually and in elaborate typography in sync with the voiceover. Another used the Dreyfus voiceover with black and white footage of 20th century icons: Albert Einstein, Martin Luther King Jr, Richard Branson, Muhammad Ali, Mohandas Gandhi, Alfred Hitchcock and Pablo Picasso were some of them.

The campaign reminded staff and customers alike of Apple's philosophy. The words are simple but brave, aspirational and inspirational, show clarity and purpose, define the company's target audience at the deep level of values and philosophy and demonstrate the confidence to break some language 'rules' — all in 101 words.

After this campaign was aired, and under Jobs' uncompromising approach, Apple went on to transform several industries and establish the company as one of the strongest brands on the planet.

You can choose your own three adjectives to describe the writing. These are mine: clear, brave, creative.

WORD, WORD, WORD...

Microsoft Word will check spelling, punctuation and grammar if you ask it to do so, and will generate suggestions on what you might want to change and readability statistics to tell you how you're doing.

This are the key points of Word's verdict about Apple, and what they mean.

Apple used roughly seven words a sentence — short and easy to read. A common average would be between 13 and 20. An average of 30+ words should set off alarm bells, as some sentences will be whoppers that are tough to get through. If you write short sentences, your work will have more impact. Apple has pulled this off, although some of these sentences are fragments, an approach normally frowned upon. Here, it works.

Apple uses short words — an average of four characters a word. These are familiar and easy to read; the text isn't bogged down in jargon and pomposity.

Apple uses no passive sentences. Good. We will delve fully into passive sentences in chapter nine, and you'll discover they have a purpose, but can throw up a red flag. For now, accept that they often give the impression of being... passive. Is that the impression you want to make?

Apple doesn't. The zero for passive sentences reflects the company's nature. Visionary, revolutionary, pioneering — not passive.

Microsoft Word's results feed into a verdict about reading ease. The higher the score, the easier the text is to read. Apple's 84.7 is a great verdict.

Word also offers a grade level that relates to the education level you need to be able to read and understand the writing. Apple's gr3.2 means the barely literate can read the company's text.

The information Word dishes out is useful as a blunt diagnostic on your writing. Long words or short? Long sentences or short? Mostly passive sentences or active ones? Easy to read? Or slow and confusing?

None of it tells you if the content is worth reading. But it gives you clues on what may, or may not, be getting in the way of your writing.

You'll find instructions on switching this feature on at the end of this chapter.

THE IMPORTANCE OF BEING ERNEST

Hemingway is a language-checking app named after Ernest Hemingway, an American novelist known for his tight, simple style.

Hemingway, the app, uses different colours to highlight long, complicated sentences and grammatical errors. You can buy and download the app for a small fee. How to interpret the colours is covered at the end of this chapter.

Hemingway loved Apple's text. Did I say

you'll never get an A+? The app highlighted only one word— the adverb *differently*. Writing guidance suggests writing with nouns and verbs, cutting adverbs where possible. It's good advice, and it's why the Hemingway app has singled out *differently*. What the software can't realise is that being *different*, even *crazy*, was Apple's goal.

Despite this quibble, Hemingway agrees with Word that you barely need to be literate to absorb Apple's text.

AND THE VERDICT FROM GRAMMARLY

The Grammarly.com website offers a more extensive check than Word or Hemingway — including a plagiarism checker along with style and vocabulary use. The site offers a free trial, after which you pay a monthly fee. Paste in your text, and the results appear.

Where Apple is concerned, Grammarly offers a harsher verdict than Word or Hemingway.

It doesn't care for Apple's punctuation and sentence structure and gives a 78/100 score that seems low for this kind of strong writing.

So what's the point of using software if you ignore or disagree with its suggestions? Computer software doesn't know the context of your writing, the impression you want to make, or the goal you want to achieve. But software pushes you to make conscious choices. And remember that you won't follow all suggestions you get from people either. Enjoy being a rebel — if it makes sense to be one.

Writing is more than a collection of language rules, a by-the-numbers craft with a set of blueprints and templates for how to write the perfect document.

It has a soul.

HORROR STORY #2 – REINVENTING THE PESTICIDE

An oil company spent hundreds of thousands of dollars developing a new pesticide, only to discover the formula had already been created five years earlier – by one of the same company's technicians. His report was so poorly written that no one had finished reading it.

GETTING SWITCHED ON

WORD

- Open Word and go to **PREFERENCES**.

- Click on **SPELLING AND GRAMMAR**.

- Tick the following boxes:

- **CHECK GRAMMAR AS YOU TYPE.**

- **CHECK GRAMMAR WITH SPELLING.**

- **SHOW READABILITY STATISTICS.**

- Beneath the readability statistics box, you will see a choice of writing style — **standard, casual, formal, technical, and custom**. Change it to suit individual pieces of writing. Make your choice and click **OK**.

- Open a document, go to the **TOOLS** menu, and then to **SPELLING AND GRAMMAR** on the drop-down menu.

- The software will check your writing. When it hits what it sees as a flaw — grammar, spelling or punctuation — it prods you to change it. You can ignore the suggestion if you wish.

- When Word finishes, a window appears showing your statistics.

These are the key areas:

Average words per sentence
If your average is fewer than 20, your sentences are within reasonable limits. However, never pass up the chance to improve and cut your sentences.

Characters per word
If your result is in double digits, you have some long, complicated words and may want to simplify them.

Passive sentences
Word prompts you to change passives because they can be a writing speed bump. Beware: the

software is sometimes wrong. We'll get to this in chapter nine.

Reading ease

Your results feed into this number; it declares if your writing is easy to read or a challenge.

These are the levels:

90-100	very easy
80-89	easy
70-79	fairly easy
60-69	standard
50-59	fairly difficult
30-49	difficult
0-29	very confusing

Change some of your language choices — shorter words, shorter sentences, and fewer passive ones — and this number goes up. It seems simple, but it is unwise to rely on the verdict. Be guided by your instincts.

HEMINGWAY

This is how Hemingway shows its results.

YELLOW　a suggestion to shorten or split a sentence.

RED　an alarm that readers may get lost before the end of a sentence.

BLUE　highlights adverbs, considered to be a sign of weak writing.

PURPLE shows a word that can be replaced with a shorter equivalent.

GREEN a passive sentence.

'You are not only responsible for what you say, but also for what you do not say.'

MARTIN LUTHER

WHAT KIND OF WRITER ARE YOU?

How do colleagues describe your work?

_____

_____

_____

_____

_____

Do these comments fit with who you feel you are? Or do they describe a different person?

_____

_____

_____

_____

_____

How would you like to change these perceptions?

_____

_____

_____

_____

_____

FAQs

So where do writing flaws come from if they aren't all from grammar, punctuation and spelling?

Most of our problems start long before we write a word. If we write without having something useful to say... if we forget our readers' needs... if we write without a plan... all of these problems show up in our language.

If I am what I write, what if I'm writing as my company — like the Apple text?

Easy. You think of your company's personality and characteristics — such as traditional or rebellious, cautious or risk taking — and you write to reflect those.

If the key to writing well lies elsewhere, why do we focus on language issues?

People love to comment on grammar, punctuation, and spelling — even when they're wrong. It's what they've been taught to do. These comments offer objective feedback, something specific and concrete we can hitch our wagons to. We have reference books or websites to support our suggestions. And improving language skills is useful. Don't ignore their value.

So why does this approach fail?

Language skills don't make you fail; ignoring everything else that leads to good writing is the speed bump. Even if you are the Obi-Wan of grammar, it won't help you to cover up a failure to think of readers' needs, gaps in your knowledge, or poor organisation. If you think language skills are all there is to good writing, you're papering over the cracks.

'I love writing, but hate starting. The page is awfully white and it says: "You may have fooled some of the people some of the time but those days are over, Giftless. I'm not your agent and I'm not your mommy: I'm a white piece of paper. You wanna dance with me?" And I really, really don't.'

AARON SORKIN

CHAPTER THREE
The dragon beneath the keyboard

NONE of us is afraid of writing. We're afraid of writing badly. We're afraid of writing nonsense while believing our work to be brilliant. We're afraid of looking stupid or grandiose, or writing something that's a career killer. We're afraid of being Jerry Maguire in the film of the same name. He is a man who writes a mission statement that loses him his job. Thank goodness for happy endings, one where Jerry Maguire's mission works and he wins the girl.

You're in good company. The highest paid and most respected writers in the world are afraid of writing badly. Awards and money don't help. Each time we face a new writing task, we are haunted by one question: can I do this well enough?

Journalists have a different fear from the one fiction writers dread. Journalists fear missing a deadline or a big story. Their sub-editors fear that their headline muse will go to a liquid lunch, never to return. They fear putting new mistakes into someone else's story while working under pressure.

If you aren't afraid of writing badly, you're either in denial or you're phoning in your work, lazily and with little thought. When you're authentic, writing is like walking naked down the street. You're entirely visible and vulnerable to criticism.

Your teachers may have said you were hopeless at writing. Perhaps you had hopes of becoming a footballer, a perfumer or an engineer and felt you would be able to avoid writing? Yet now, even if you have a traditionally non-writing career, your life is full of it. The world has changed and writing is compulsory. Who knew?

Luckily, I always knew writing would be fundamental in my life. When I'm clear about why I'm writing, who I'm writing for, and I am confident in what I have to say and how best to say it, then the words flow. I am 'in the zone' channelling the words through my fingers without fear.

When my mind is mush, I write just as much crap as anyone else and with just as much fear.

Authors of books — fiction or non-fiction — have editors pushing them to be clear and concise. Journalists have Miles Kington's diamond cutting sub-editors chipping away at everything people shouldn't be asked to read until once convoluted stories sparkle.

No one writes superbly without help. Everyone needs a diamond cutter and you'll find out how to recruit yours in chapter 14.

When you grapple with fear you may have to go over old language skills, but it's just old ground. Even if the quadratic equations that baffled me at school have stayed the same, our language and the way we use it has moved on.

HORROR STORY #3 – THROWING AWAY A FORTUNE

In a survey of Fortune 500 companies, HR professionals reported throwing away a candidate's CV for as few as one or two errors in grammar or spelling.

THE PROCRASTINATION TRAP

WHEN we avoid tackling our fear, we procrastinate and stay stuck. Often, we pretend we're doing something important. Sometimes we procrastinate with good reason, because we're not ready to write. Mostly, it's fear.

Here are some of the things we say and do to avoid writing;

I'm tired
I'm too tired to write anything good. I'll produce crap. I'll do something else until I have more energy. I could go to a meeting and tune out, mulling over what I'm going to write when I have the energy. I'll start tomorrow.

I'm hungry
I need a biscuit or two before I write. Lunch would be better. I'll only have one glass of wine to avoid a mid-afternoon slump. Perhaps I'd better start tomorrow when I'm fresher? I'll get so much done after a healthy breakfast.

I'm thirsty
How can I coax my muse into turning up if I'm dehydrated? Herbal tea is a better choice than coffee. Muses are probably health nuts. Trouble is, I'll have to buy herbal tea. But my body is a temple, and I want powerful thoughts to come tumbling onto the keyboard instead of being dragged out with pliers. I'll buy herbal tea on the way home, and start tomorrow.

I need to tidy my desk
A cluttered space reflects a cluttered mind. I'll write crap if I'm surrounded by crap. I should declutter my office and tidy my computer too. Perhaps Feng Shui research might help me to reorganise my space and channel my energy. I'll start writing tomorrow with my Chi in place.

I need to tidy my house
Working from home has removed all office distractions — apart from phone calls and

emails — but the cluttered space rule applies here too. My muse won't come to an untidy house. Once I've emptied the dishwasher and the washing machine, finished the ironing and cleaned my son's room, I'll have the tidiness I need in which to give birth to world-changing ideas. I'll write tomorrow.

I need to go for a walk
The state of my son's room is hijacking my focus. If I take a short break, and do breathing exercises as I walk, my mind will clear and I'll become inspired. I can collect the dry cleaning on the way back and stop off at the bank. Two jobs out of the way before I write. I'll start tomorrow.

I need to make some phone calls
Disruptions stop my flow, so I'll call my mum, sister, the members of my book club, and then register with the telephone preference service to head off sales calls. I'll put a notice on the front door to deter religious groups. I wonder if the local print shop can do a laminated sign that shows I mean business? I'll be ready to write tomorrow.

I need to check my social media
I may be tired, thirsty and angry about my family's untidiness, but great thoughts are ready to burst forth. I'll check Facebook, Twitter, and my emails before switching off all alerts. I can't miss anything vital while I'm writing. I'll put the TV on mute, but leave it on a news channel. I can't have inspired thoughts if I'm not tuned

into the modern world. I can keep one eye on the TV while I'm writing.

I could go to the coffee shop

I didn't realise my neighbours had builders working on their house. The kids will be home soon and they might want help with homework or, worse, want a cooked meal. And our needy cat is sitting on the keyboard, demanding attention. If we had a dog, I could take it for a walk and do some powerful thinking while I'm out.

We each have our favourite ways of procrastinating and often accomplish useful stuff. Trouble is, little of it is writing. Avoiding disruptions and having a clear workspace help us to produce good writing. But getting our houses Feng Shued does not get business reports and client proposals written.

I've been known to leave my desk and head into the street, certain I could hear the wailing of a cat trapped in a tree, only to discover the distraction to be a bird skilled at trapped-cat mimicry.

But I believe I own the most extreme procrastination story I've ever come across. I heard a harrowing real life story and decided to turn it into a film script. It involved an ex-SAS officer who worked in Croatia during the newly formed country's fight to separate from Serbia in the early 1990s. The heart of the story was about a war atrocity being covered up to avoid derailing peace talks. It was horrifying material and I was fired up with outrage at the story being buried. The decision to tackle it felt like a no-brainer as I'd written film scripts before.

At the same time, I was involved in a debate about a small company's future. Without new money being injected, the company would fail; my experience and instincts told me that letting the company go under was for the best. But no one should make that kind of decision without knowing the facts.

So I threw myself into analysing the company's situation. I downloaded company accounts as far back as the start-up, read copious emails about prospective new business and previous sales, trawled through intellectual property agreements, and pulled in favours to get a professional view of the company's history and prospects.

I wrote my socks off and did a damned fine job. The shareholders thanked me for my work and took action. Would I have plunged so deeply into my analysis without the film script waiting to be written? Probably not. I wrote partly to procrastinate about writing something that scared me.

It was a war story. What did I know about war? I had no experience as a soldier and I had never been a war reporter. My work would be trite, lacking in authenticity, insulting to those whose story it was. I would be ridiculed, humiliated. It would ruin my screenwriting career.

I would never work again...

But I was a journalist, one with a reasonable

background in financial reporting. Why not stay in my comfort zone and look into a company's future instead? I was unlikely to meet any of the fearsome quadratic equations that terrified me, and that was a bonus.

Ultimately, I was called to account for the lack of progress on the film script. I confronted my fear and buckled down to writing. The script won a prize in a story competition, and is in development.

Recognise your procrastination tactics and deal with them. It's likely that you're afraid of being judged. There's a lot you don't know and you're afraid to find out how much that is. You can't think of a single idea worth sharing. People will discover that you're unfit to keep your job. You'll be putting your head above a parapet and you'd rather it wasn't shot at. Better to stay hidden.

These thoughts are killers, if you allow them to take hold.

Try some tactics to help you to push through procrastination.

- Ask yourself what's the worst that might happen if your writing fails? Be realistic. How likely is it to happen, particularly if you plunge in with vigour?

- Ask if you're stuck with good reason. Do you have research gaps? Are you confused about why you need to write? Do you know enough about your readers? Are you following a complicated structure that needs simplifying?

- Allow yourself to write rubbish. No one else has to see your first draft.

- Are you afraid to ruffle feathers with new ideas, while hating the thought of churning out the same old stuff? Clear, direct writing is not the same as 'shock and awe'. You don't have to raze anything to the ground to nudge the world.

- If you're stuck on the first sentence, write the second one. Or the second paragraph. No commandment says: 'Thou must start at the beginning'. Start with an easy section that gets you moving. Start somewhere... even if you throw it away later.

- Shift your focus onto your readers and what they need. When people read, they want to find out what's in it for them. Few are waiting for you to trip up.

- Think about your long-term goals. How will your career develop if you write well? How can your writing help your company? Your industry? Take this as far as you can; it will get you moving.

- Go to the loo, get something to eat or drink, and then shut the door. Switch off everything but the air supply. Don't book any Feng Shui experts.

- Do some deep breathing, or a quick meditation... find your favourite way to empty your head. This is only procrastination if it becomes an end in itself.

- Avoid or ignore people who declare that it's not worth putting in major effort, that it's best to deliver only what people expect. If you were happy to limit your writing, you wouldn't be reading this book. Writing mentor Julia Cameron calls these people 'crazymakers', people who share comments or invitations to pull you off track. Long lunches. Shopping sprees. Don't succumb and become your own crazymaker.

It takes a lot of time, energy and excuses not to write. Is it worth all of that effort to achieve — nothing?

'Writing is the dragon that lives underneath my floorboards. The one I incessantly feed for fear it may turn and devour my ass.'

QUENTIN R BUFOGLE

FAQS

Is fear this big a deal?

It often is. Anything that can change the world is scary, particularly when we're trying to do it well. What if we screw up? Will the sky fall in? Chances are you won't screw up and the sky will stay where it is. Refusing to try is the failure.

I've been bungee jumping, white water rafting and walked over hot coals. Do you really think I'm afraid of a few words?

Yes, you're afraid of getting those words wrong. Didn't bungee jumping teach you anything? If you're not afraid, you're playing it safe. Clear, direct writing is... naked. We have nowhere to hide, and it's scary. People might not like what we say or think we're dumb. These thoughts keep us in our comfort zone. We think that's safe, but it isn't. Get out there and write. No one else will express the same thoughts exactly the way that you do. If you don't do it, that's a permanent loss.

Why can't we get rid of the fear permanently?

If we banished it, we'd be back in our comfort zone, playing it safe. The only way to be safe is to stand out and be ourselves.

Won't my fear disappear if I brush up my grammar, punctuation and spelling?

No. Language skills are important, but we need more if we're to write well. We need to build a strong writing purpose and a connection with our readers. We need clear thinking based on knowledge and creative insights. We need a writing plan along with feedback that pushes us to do better. If we start with a muddle, good grammar won't cover it up.

FIGHTING FEAR

Name three fears that get in the way of your writing.

_____

_____

_____

_____

Name three of your favourite procrastination tactics.

_____

_____

_____

_____

What would be the advantage of dropping them?

_____

_____

_____

_____

'Writing is like making love. Don't worry about the orgasm, just concentrate on the process.'

ISABEL ALLENDE

CHAPTER FOUR

Why 'process' seems to be the hardest word

ASK people what makes writing 'bad' and you'll hear predictable tirades about the lost arts of spelling, grammar, punctuation and the prevailing lack of attention to detail. These rants, often about an imagined, golden age of education, will be well meant, impassioned, and sometimes include a comedy moment or two. They make a strong case; at the same time, they miss the big picture.

Plenty of Amazon's 65,000-plus book titles on writing skills focus on spelling, grammar and punctuation. Yet they haven't stopped the flow of bad writing. Writing websites follow a similar pattern and focus on language skills. Facebook has several pages featuring funny posts from the grammar police. Where you once got away with a private C- on your work, now you get publicly pilloried. All of this is useful, but limited.

Writing is a process, something we can learn and repeat with equal chance of success on each occasion. It helps to reduce the fog in our minds and the element of writing luck. Process gives us a touchstone to guide us through moments of confusion, guesswork and insecurity because our approach is geared towards clarity of thought. We open up space for good writing to emerge.

Using a process allows us to split writing into steps, and pushes us to focus on doing each stage well. We stop trying to multitask our way through writing, an approach that generates mediocre results.

'A tremendous amount of evidence shows that the brain does better when it's performing tasks in sequence, rather than all at once,' said the late Clifford Nass, a professor of communications at Stanford University. He's not the only one to nail multitasking as a problem.

A study funded by Hewlett Packard and conducted by the Institute of Psychiatry at the University of London found that distractions of email and phone calls can make our IQs drop more than twice as much than if we were smoking marijuana.

And our headless chicken behaviour even made news with the publication of *The Distraction Trap*, by Frances Booth. The book offers guidance in ditching our multitasking addiction and regaining our focus.

In fact, we're kidding ourselves that we're actually multitasking, when we're really task switching. This may sound better, but isn't.

Guy Winch, author of *Emotional First Aid: Practical Strategies for Treating Failure, Rejection, Guilt and Other Everyday Psychological Injuries*, says: 'Moving back and forth between several tasks actually wastes productivity because your attention is expended on the act of switching gears — plus you never get fully "in the zone" for either activity.' The shocker, according to some researchers, is that task switching may cut our productivity by as much as 40 per cent.

So multitasking makes us slow and dumb at the same time — a rotten combination. The answer is simple: stop doing it.

Checking emails, Facebook and Twitter, taking phone calls, and surfing the web — these all have to go into the dustbin while we're writing. We need to learn to refocus our attention. It may ruffle feathers among colleagues used to having you on tap at the ping of a digital alert. That is their problem, not yours.

But there's more to successful writing than dropping our addiction to our multitasking delusion. Focusing on one step at a time is great, but we need our steps in the right order. There's no point worrying about the structure of documents before we've worked out why we're writing in the first place. Obsessing about grammar before working out our readers' needs is equally bad. Editing and proofing before we've finished essential research is... yes, it's dumb.

Messy results reflect our state of mind. We hop between writing stages, losing clarity of thought instead of freeing our minds to produce creative results.

Bummer.

HORROR STORY #4 – WHEREFORE ART THOU, DICTIONARY?

Clothing chain Topshop commissioned a William Shakespeare-inspired women's T-shirt, using the line 'Romeo, Romeo, wherefore art thou Romeo?' The famous quote was attributed to Shakespere, not Shakespeare. The mistake was spotted only after the £20 T-shirts went on sale, prompting an expensive recall.

SO WHERE DO I START?

Once you've switched off social media alerts, emails, unplugged the phone and hung a DO NOT DISTURB sign where no one can miss it, you're on the road to writing well. If you're a multitasker extraordinaire, changing your default position may feel as if you've dropped off the edge of the world.

Your best thinking has got you to a B-list level of writing, maybe lower. So persevere with the new approach. If you want a seat at the A-list table with the cool kids who decide how the world is run, you'll need to unpick some ingrained habits. Writing that rocks the world is worth the effort.

What comes next is simple and logical, but far from superficial. The steps are the same if you're writing a one-page letter or a 50-page report. With a short document you'll be able to bounce through most of these steps in your head. But you'll still be using the process. And this kind of hop, skip and jump through the process is good practice for the more elaborate way you'll handle long-form writing.

This is the brief version of what we'll discover in part two.

PURPOSE

Work out what you want your writing to achieve and why. Not just for you, your career, and your company's success. Not just for awards and honours. Don't stop at the obvious. Bring in your readers and their purpose, even goals they haven't realised they can achieve. Between you, you're aiming to nudge the world a little — or a lot.

READERS

You want readers hooked and hanging onto your every word. If you don't know who they are, and how to connect with them, your readers are likely to stray. And if you don't know who they are and what they want, how do you know what they *need* to read?

RESEARCH

Research is a mini process in itself. You ask smart and challenging questions, dig up lots of answers, and allow yourself to stray. You digest everything and allow new ideas to bubble up. The more you discover, the more you can share and the more people are likely to listen. Become a research junkie. You know it makes sense.

STRUCTURE

We all love it when a plan comes together. And there's no point in starting to write without a plan. Your plan doesn't have to be long, and for a short document, you probably won't even have to write it down. Whatever the length, your writing needs to be organised in a way that makes sense for your purpose and for your readers.

WRITING

When you know what you're trying to achieve... who you're writing for... have lots of insights to share... and a solid plan for how to show your ideas — this is where your language skills come front and centre. Now you can focus on the perfect way to capture what you need to say; you'll discover you know more about skilful use of language than you imagined.

While the grammar of language is important, remember that writing is personal. It's about you and your ideas, and this is where you should concentrate on the impression you want to make. As your confidence grows, you may even decide to break some grammar 'rules' when it works for your purpose.

REWRITING AND EDITING

No one writes a perfect first draft, and everyone needs feedback. In an earlier chapter, I wanted you to choose people to help you discover your writing identity. Now you want helpers to give you forensic editing and proofreading feedback. This is about improving specific pieces of writing. The trick is knowing how to get useful feedback, when to listen, and when to stick to your instincts.

Tackling writing in a process-led way involves phases where left-brain and right-brain activity take turns to dominate. You mix periods of creativity and *Eureka!* moments with others where you analyse and push your ideas. Write with the heart. Edit with your head.

Aside from losing your insecurities about your writing weaknesses, there are many upsides.

You think more clearly
Splitting writing into a process creates a clear mind and room for creative thought. You solve a tough business problem in a new way that hasn't occurred to anyone. You find an innovative way to boost sales. You identify an approach that excites clients and raises their ambitions.

Your writing improves
When you focus on each stage of the process, your writing develops a 'wow' factor. Armed with a deep purpose, you start writing for more than a salary — and it shows. You'll enjoy writing more. Why wouldn't you? You're focused and clear.

Your confidence grows

Is your document OK? Did you miss crucial points? Will your language skills embarrass you? Will anything come back to bite you? These doubts disappear as your writing anxiety fades.

When you don't have a good reason for formulaic writing — and there isn't one — a gremlin eats away at your confidence. Inside, you always knew there wasn't a formula...

You head off problems early and save time

No one is perfect, even with a process as your touchstone. Your thinking may drift. You may miss useful research. You may lose sight of your readers. Your plans stray off-piste. You struggle to find the right words. But you won't hit all of these snags at once, the way you have in the past. Pitfalls become obvious earlier, when it's easier to fix them. Writing in an organised way gets the job done more quickly— and with fewer heart attacks.

People will turn to you for advice

Who doesn't want a reputation as a world-class expert on grammar? Having a process as your guide can turn you into the writing guru everyone likes to consult. You still need to ask for feedback. Everyone needs a sounding board, even if you have become the writing master.

These upsides sound ambitious and a bit fabulous, and they are. But your aim is simple: push someone out of your seat at the A-list writing table so you can start nudging the world.

'Creativity is just connecting things. When you ask creative people how they did something, they feel a little guilty because they didn't really do it, they just saw something.'

STEVE JOBS

FAQs

So grammar and punctuation aren't that important?

Seriously? Of course they're important. But there's a lot to do before you start pulling sentences together, so they will feel less intimidating by the time you get to them. You don't need to be an expert on grammar and punctuation to write well, but you have to have a healthy level of expertise to express yourself clearly. So you didn't get it at school? Deal with it.

Surely it can't be this easy?

Who said it was easy? Simplicity is a hard concept to pull off. Writing is hard...and there's no reason why it should be otherwise. You've only read the mini version of what's to come in part two. Read on, and you'll discover the full picture.

FROM START TO FINISH

What percentage of your writing time do you spend on the following steps?

Working out your writing purpose.

_____

_____

Thinking of readers and what they need.

_____

_____

Doing research.

_____

_____

Outlining and structure.

_____

_____

Writing.

_____

_____

Editing and rewriting.

_____

_____

Which area gives you most trouble? Why?

_____

_____

_____

Where are you strongest? Why?

_____

_____

_____

Are there areas where you spend no time at all?
Why?

_____

_____

_____

PART TWO

Step by step: how the
process works

'Writing is not magic. It's a craft, a process, a set of steps. As with any process, things sometimes break down. So the act of writing always includes problem solving.'

ROY PETER CLARK

'Good writing does not succeed or fail on the strength of its ability to persuade. It succeeds or fails on the strength of its ability to engage you, to make you think, to give you a glimpse into someone else's head.'

MALCOLM GLADWELL

'The best way to become acquainted with a subject is to write about it.'

BENJAMIN DISRAELI

'People don't buy what you do; they buy why you do it.'

SIMON SINEK

CHAPTER FIVE

So you want to change the world?

IT'S easy to lose the point of writing in a world where we are awash with the stuff. And technology makes it easier than ever before to pin down some words and ping them out, hoping to rock the world.

The deluge of words we face is relentless, even compulsory. We have to contribute if we want to stand out in this sea of writing. It's astonishing any other work gets done because when we're not writing, we're reading or sleeping. And while we sleep, writing piles up from people who are awake and typing on the other side of the world.

Death is no excuse for slacking. One of my favourite authors — the detective writer Raymond Chandler — still posts on Facebook and he died in 1959.

It's a world gone mad.

We post our lives on social media; we write to sell things on eBay; we dish up online reviews about products we've bought, restaurants we've visited, films we've watched and holidays we've loved and hated. We sign petitions about government policies and business practices we feel are wrong.

In business, we write to boost sales and win contracts, to ask or answer questions, to turn aggrieved customers into fans, to analyse problems and propose what we hope are sensible solutions. We share our expertise, we teach and aim to influence. We even hope to entertain.

We are all on a writing treadmill, even if words are a by-product of 'proper' jobs, where writing would seem to be a luxury. Yet perfumers blog about their creations, and personal trainers tweet about getting fit. Engineers write for as much as 30 per cent of their working day instead of creating the next phase of the modern world in their workshops.

We write on trains, in hotels and coffee shops, even while walking along busy pavements bumping into other pedestrians.

Is it any wonder that we've lost the point of why we write?

SO WHAT *IS* THE POINT?

Research shows that we work better when we find purpose to our work, a meaning that goes beyond money. The behavioural scientist Dan Ariely has evidence that we are driven not primarily by money but by having meaningful work, by being acknowledged for our work and by how tough it is to do it. The harder it is to excel at our work, the prouder we feel when we finish it. We need money to live, but we need meaning to live well.

If you have deep meaning at the heart of your writing — and it's there if you look for it — you are on your way to better writing. The love of writing may not be what gets you out of bed each day; your true passions in life may lie elsewhere, perhaps in science, fashion, technology, engineering, or as a brand-building entrepreneur.

When you accept the idea that writing helps you to stand out in your true calling, you'll be motivated to write well. You'll recognise it as a tool you can harness in the pursuit of a passion that's more important to you.

Purpose can be general and still act as a powerful motivator, and it isn't hard to find if you look deeper than we're used to doing on a daily basis. Take a simple example: MIND THE GAP. It's a warning we see and take for granted on underground and rail platforms. Cynics will claim the warning's purpose, particularly in our litigious age, to be a legal or insurance one. But this is a superficial meaning; the deeper one is to save lives and avoid injuries.

As you search, you may find a purpose for your readers that hasn't even occurred to them. In *My Fair Lady*, the musical film version of George Bernard Shaw's play *Pygmalion*, Eliza Doolittle wants to learn 'to talk proper' so she can get a job in a flower shop, instead of selling on the corner of Tottenham Court Road. Her accent and command of English aren't up to scratch and linguistics expert Professor Henry Higgins takes on the task of teaching her to speak well. It goes badly. Eliza just doesn't get it.

When she's on the cusp of giving up, Higgins gives Eliza a purpose beyond a job in a flower shop. 'Just think what you're dealing with,' says Higgins. 'The majesty and grandeur of the English language. It's the greatest possession we have. The noblest thoughts that ever flowed through the hearts of men are contained in its extraordinary, imaginative and musical mixtures of sounds. And that's what you've set yourself out to conquer, Eliza. And conquer it you will.'

Eliza is stunned. This goal hadn't remotely appeared on her radar. But now she understands. Moments later, her voice is fluid and eloquent. She rises to the challenge, stretching herself past the mechanics of voice. Eliza sets out with a small goal but rises to a bigger challenge offered by someone with a grand vision.

It's fiction, of course, because fiction has to make more sense than real life. But fiction also has to resonate with us and be credible.

Persist with a powerful purpose in your own life and you have a chance not just of engaging with readers, but also of raising their sights.

> **HORROR STORY #5 – SO THERE REALLY IS A GRAMMAR CEILING?**
>
> A study of 100 LinkedIn profiles of native English speakers found those who'd failed to reach director-level positions within the first ten years of their careers made two-and-a-half times as many grammar mistakes as their director-level colleagues.
>
> In the same study, professionals with six to nine career promotions made 45 per cent fewer grammatical errors than colleagues promoted between one and four times.

A WORLD CHANGING CRAFT

The idea of using words to change the world may seem grandiose. Yet it works. Writing gets change moving, sometimes quietly and sometimes with a fanfare.

> *We hold these truths to be self-evident that all men are created equal, that they are endowed by their Creator with certain unalienable Rights, that among these are life, Liberty and the pursuit of Happiness.*

These may be dusty words for our modern tastes, particularly since they're too long for a tweet, but these 35 words from the American Declaration of Independence form one of the most influential sentences in the English language. Not only are they a touchstone for an entire nation of the moral standard it strives to uphold, but other nations have also adapted these words and imported their values into their own constitutions. Proof that only 35 words can pack a powerful punch.

British history has its equivalent in the Magna Carta. Confronted by rebellious barons outraged at abuses of the justice system and exploitation of feudal rights, King John was pressed into agreeing to limit his royal authority and to accept that the king was subject to the law, not above it. He signed the Magna Carta. The most famous section, still valid, is this:

No free man shall be seized or imprisoned, or stripped of his rights or possessions, or outlawed or exiled — nor will we proceed with force against him — except by the lawful judgement of his equals or by the law of the land. To no one will we sell, to no one deny or delay right or justice.

Look past the dated style and you'll find no-nonsense purpose that left King John no room to backtrack. It's why this clause still matters, even with a style that doesn't fit with our digital age.

Writing defines our laws, holds people to account, rallies causes, topples dictators, incites revolutions and spreads ideas. On a personal and business level, it can build a strong career and help transform a company into a world-class brand. The Apple example shows the impact that comes with purpose. In our digital age, well-crafted words have a reach beyond the imagination of the American founding fathers or the barons who confronted King John.

Most touchingly, writing has been a prescription for healing. Jane Austen's novels were given to shell-shocked soldiers in World War One because of their soothing quality, says Dr Paula Byrne — author of *The Real Jane Austen: A Life in Small Things*, and a fellow of Harris Manchester College, Oxford. Byrne believes Austen's work offered comfort in a crazy world and explains why her books have lasting appeal. 'She was read in the trenches,' says Byrne. 'She was a prescribed script for tortured, troubled souls.'

How do we harness this clout? I imagine you already have a nagging voice nibbling away at your insides, sneering about who you think you are to want to nudge the world. You, who only got a C- in English. Where on earth could you find the space to form a new nation? Why don't you dream smaller? And there's nothing wrong with that, unless you want bigger.

Remind the carping voice that language skills aren't the speed bump you've always thought them to be. Right now you're tackling purpose, working out a meaning that will drive you to write well.

WRITING IS THINKING

Writing is a physical link from your brain to the outside world, showing who you are to anyone who reads your work. It shows how you think and how you act. The trouble is, if you can't think well, you can't share what you know. And that limits your power to nudge the world more than any flaws in your grammar.

So your first step should be to think clearly about your purpose, and that means pushing beyond easy answers.

Writing a book has to carry an author through the long months leading to publication, including the days when they are tired and it feels like a slog. They still have to turn up and write.

So what is my purpose in writing this book? Helping readers to create first-class brands and companies, winning finance and solving problems along the way... offering people tools that help them get elected to public office... giving entrepreneurs the tools to reinvent industries... improving the skills of those who want social reform... this is ambitious purpose.

Smaller goals will crop up along the way where good writing is a killer asset. Getting an interview for a new job... pitching for a contract... analysing why a project succeeded or failed... even getting past the first hurdle on a dating site... each goal builds into something bigger.

Thinking about readers and their ambitions has shaped the content, length and style of this book, because I want particular readers, people who write as a means to an end; an end that gives them greater joy.

You may be driven by building a better

mousetrap that becomes a world-class success. I'm driven by showing you how writing well helps you to reach your goal.

Purpose keeps you on track, now and during the steps that follow.

HORROR STORY #6 – THE $2M COMMA

In October 2006 a contract dispute between Canadian cable company Rogers Communications and telephone company Bell Aliant boiled down to the placing of a comma. Bell Aliant won the case and was able to save more than $2m by ending the contract early.

ASKING THE RIGHT QUESTIONS

Building writing purpose means asking searching questions and seeing how far you can push them. What will writing do for me, and my company? What will it do for my industry readers, clients or investors?

Imagine that you need to come up with a new direction for a tired brand. Writing a proposal and winning agreement for it is the smallest purpose you have: a short-term goal. Deeper meaning comes from the long-term ripples of this success.

If your plan shows clear thinking and becomes a success, you may have helped to create new jobs, a boost for your company — and the wider economy.

Success shows in your confidence and your CV, helping you to a better job in the future, or a promotion where you already work. When a similar need looms again, who will your bosses turn to?

The reputation of your boss grows since they picked the right person for a crucial task. They earn a promotion, perhaps taking you with them. Or they go to another company and want you to join them. Or their vacant job comes to you.

In time, you, your colleagues and clients move on. The financial returns you helped to create will be used elsewhere, perhaps creating jobs and prosperity you aren't even aware of.

Sometime in the future, people *will* take your calls. Why? Because your strong sense of purpose showed up in your writing — and it's become part of your reputation.

The benefits of good writing aren't confined to you. But they start with your purpose and words. One successful document is a step to building long-term influence. Others may focus purely on short-term goals — what you might call a dirty win. Long-term purpose pays off better.

Of course, your successful brand strategy needs to be executed with care. But nailing your purpose makes this more likely, since clear writing becomes the touchstone for action.

When you recognise the responsibility your writing carries, and the long-term influence you can build, you will dig deeper into research, ask and answer tough questions, and devise a clear plan.

You'll do most of this hard work before you've written a word.

You will already be a better writer.

'If people cannot write well, they cannot think well, and if they cannot think well, others will do their thinking for them.'

GEORGE ORWELL

FAQs

Must I want to change the world just to write better?

Changing the world doesn't have to mean overthrowing a government, and nudging the world appears in unexpected ways. Maybe your writing helps to finance and make a film. Lots of freelance filmmakers get paid to do what they're good at, the film gets released, and people sit in cinemas all over the world, and laugh — in a good way. They may have lost their jobs, be worried about their families, or they may be seriously ill. You were part of the team that helped people to forget their troubles for a short while. Doesn't that nudge the world a little? How great would this make you feel?

I get it. But what's wrong with taking it one small step at a time?

Nothing. In fact, you'll have to take it step by step. But thinking of the big things that come from small steps will motivate you to write well. We work better when we feel we make a difference.

Now that I realise how much impact writing can have, I'm even more scared. Is there a pill I can take to remove the pressure?
Er, no. Your writing is important whether you are aware of it or not. When you realise how powerful writing is, you have a reason to become more skilled at it. Don't lose the plot and think it's all about you. Your writing is part of a big picture that includes other people and *their* passions.

What if I write really well and someone else gets all the credit?
Be gracious. If you write well repeatedly — and the process takes away the chance of success being a fluke — your work *will* get noticed. What's the alternative? Writing badly out of spite? You're in this for the long game, not a dirty win.

WHAT'S YOUR POINT?

Consider a long-form document you've already written — maybe a business pitch, project update or analysis, strategy review, business plan — and answer these questions.

Did you take the document's purpose beyond the short term?

_____

_____

_____

_____

How could you have thought longer-term about purpose?

_____

_____

_____

_____

How would this have given you greater drive to write better?

_____

_____

_____

_____

'Those who write clearly have readers; those who write obscurely have commentators.'

ALBERT CAMUS

CHAPTER SIX

Getting to know your imaginary friends

WRITING is not a narcissistic activity that's all about what you want to say. It's a two-way conversation between you and your readers, except that readers are busy people, doing something else while you write.

Consider what your readers' working day looks like. They share similar challenges to the ones you face. They're overwhelmed on occasion, and often feel time-poor. They have writing of their own to tackle. You may be lucky: they may read your work as a procrastination tactic, but don't count on it.

Imagine the diversions that may hijack their day... a flu epidemic sweeps the office and creates staff shortages... a computer system breakdown causes mayhem... volcanic ash disrupts the travel plans of key personnel on their way to a meeting... a client brings forward a deadline... an email screams for an answer.

What are the chances of their finding time to read your work? If you have a reputation for C-writing, what are the chances they'll want to?

This sounds harsh since your purpose is to help them achieve their goals. The trouble is, we all want clear, direct writing, until we're the writer... and then we want someone to cut us some slack.

Remember that readers are your lifeblood; without them, you are toast. It makes sense to show them some respect. So here are some home truths you may want to tattoo on your soul.

Readers don't have to read anything

This may sound like heresy, but we all filter and prioritise. We dump documents into the bin without reading a word. Our lives may be poorer for not reading them and later we may wish we hadn't been so dismissive. But it's rarely fatal when we don't read. It's a rookie mistake to assume that our readers will plough through poor writing. They won't.

People may start reading, but no one has to finish

None of us works in a bubble where we can ring-fence our reading time. When did you last read an entire news story or blog? Did you stop because you were bored? Were you distracted or reading on the train and reached your station? Did someone announce that dinner was ready? Or was your bath getting cold? We have other calls on our time.

Readers don't have to reread anything

Clarity is *your* mission. If your writing is hard to understand when someone first reads it, they may not give you a second chance.

Readers don't have to look up words

Your role is to engage and communicate, not to educate readers by using long-winded words they have to look up. Driving readers to a dictionary means they've stopped reading your work. This usually drives them towards someone who writes more simply.

Readers don't have to search for buried answers

Being asked questions you've already answered in your writing is annoying. You may have a bad writing structure and have your answers in the wrong place. Treat questions as a gift. Answer them and write more coherently the next time. Of course, someone may be pretending to have read your work when they didn't have the time or inclination. Remind yourself that no one needs to read a word.

Readers don't have to agree with you

You're trying to engage readers, not form a cult following whose only job is to say yes. Good writing organises your thoughts, so you'll be ready for a debate. Of course, if people unreservedly jump on the bus you're driving, just give them a ticket — and drive.

> ## HORROR STORY #7 – MAKING GRAMMAR A GOOD HABIT
>
> Forbes has identified poor grammar as one of 13 habits that can cost someone their job. Curiously, murder isn't one of the other 12.

WHO ARE THESE GUYS?

So who are your readers? You write to people, not to an email address, a company or public body, and never to a demographic group. Your readers are people who sometimes go to the cinema or theatre, have romantic dinners that lead to sex, have books to read from their favourite genres, and often have children who prompt family squabbles. They may have weird choices of wallpaper and love cookery programmes on TV. They may be hooked on video games or the gym. You may be writing to someone just like you, or someone who is chalk to your cheese. Someone you already know, or someone you have yet to meet.

You need to form a picture of who they are and what they want.

How do your readers earn a living?

It makes sense to start by fleshing out what your readers do for work. But don't fall into the trap of thinking that accountants and lawyers are all dull people who love jargon and boring writing. Hairdressers are more than people with an 'Are you going anywhere nice on holiday?' icebreaker. Taxi drivers don't always know how to run the country. Murderers sometimes help old ladies across the road.

Take a look at some TED talks for a fresh look at people and how they approach their jobs. You'll find scientists with a quirky sense of humour and creatives who can be pompous. I've seen a scientist end a TED talk with a sword-swallowing trick that brought the house down with good reason. TED can turn you on to subjects you thought would be boring, all because passionate people have a way of grabbing attention and keeping it.

How old are your readers?

Age is more than a number, particularly where writing is concerned. Young people aren't all fun-loving any more than old people are all grumpy. Young people may be saving for a deposit on a house and less open to spending. Or they may be carefree and living for the moment.

Old people may be closed off to new ideas and have one foot in the grave. Or they may be splashing the cash and ticking off items on their bucket list. They may even be one of an increasing number of oldies starting a new business.

Pigeonholing on the basis of age exposes the pitfall that readers may not get your jokes or time-specific references. Cultural and historical points of reference change with age, experience and knowledge that comes only with years.

One day, my stepson asked how my working day had been. Work was fun, I said, while adding that I was sad at the news of Katharine Hepburn's death.

'Who's Katharine Hepburn?' was the response that stunned me, particularly since I'd made my stepson sit through at least three of her films. A famous actress. A four-time Oscar winner. Then I came up with the clincher. 'She was the Meryl Streep of her day.' When 'Who's Meryl Streep?' came back at me, I gave up.

Be careful of cultural or historical references that leave your readers puzzled. This section has the heading 'WHO ARE THESE GUYS?', a line of dialogue from the film *Butch Cassidy and the Sundance Kid*. It works even if you haven't seen the film.

What do your readers already know?
If you fail to consider what your readers already know, how do you know when your writing offers something fresh and exciting? Something readers haven't already dismissed?

If your readers already have background knowledge, you can demonstrate some of yours as a section that can be skipped over by those in the know. Alternatively, you can bring in some background as a brief aside to your ideas, showing that you too have come from a sensible starting point.

At the end of this book, you'll find a small example of how to do this in *B is for — background.*

What level of education do your readers have?

Intelligence is not the issue here since exams are too limited a way of assessing it. Many highly intelligent people did badly in formal education yet moved on to change the world. And highly educated people can be underachievers with an inflated view of their smarts.

People with poor academic results may feel inferior and avoid asking what they feel are 'stupid' questions. A 'frequently asked questions' section may avoid an unhelpful silence, although that's not the only reason for using this kind of structural device. And you may find these non-academic people may be bolshie world-changers happy to challenge the status quo. They may be both at different times.

What else do your readers read?

Which newspapers and magazines do your readers buy and read for pleasure or to add to their general knowledge? Knowing your readers' personal reading choices offers clear hints on how to approach them.

If they buy *The Sun* newspaper it tells us they like short, pithy sentences and small bites of information, corralled into short, tightly organised sections. *The Sun* uses active writing that gets to the point and stops as soon as the job is done.

We may choose to offer these readers short bursts of writing in distinct sections — because that's the style they're already paying for. Don't delude yourself that this choice makes your writing easier. Journalists and sub-editors who work for *The Sun* are respected by their peers; it takes tremendous skill to write with that level of brevity and clarity.

If your readers buy *The Financial Times*, then we can stretch the length of sentences and even the document as a whole, simply because that's what the FT offers its readers. It's the style they're already paying for.

The rookie mistake is to feel entitled to talk down to *The Sun*'s readers with the misguided idea that they aren't knowledgeable or interested in anything other than showbiz gossip. Nor does it give me permission to pontificate at great length, using lots of jargon, to FT readers on the assumption that they're financial know-alls.

How rich are your readers?
Any element of your readers' lives gives you a fuller picture of their likely wants and needs. Sometimes that picture comes in surprising ways.

When the UK government introduced the Enterprise Investment Scheme as a way of enticing wealthy people to invest in small businesses, publicity majored on the tax incentives available to investors. For instance, anyone investing through an EIS scheme would gain 20 per cent tax relief to offset against income tax. It sounds likely to make fundraising easy.

But... if you major on this advantage, you'll have missed the fact that this is less attractive for people rich enough to live off company dividends, since these are taxable in a different way.

There's wealthy... and there's wealthy. Which group does your potential investor fall into?

The more you know about your readers and their interests, the easier writing becomes. Questions about what to include or exclude become no-brainers to answer. Decisions on how to structure your writing become easier to make. Language choices fall into place with ease.

Writing stops being general and becomes focused. You have far more chance of connecting and engaging with your readers — because you know who they are...

'It's the first thing I tell my students: if you could understand, really understand, that no one needs to read your work, then your writing would improve vastly by the time we meet in this classroom again.'

DAN BARDEN

FAQs

Doesn't knowing this much about readers make life more complicated?

Far from it. The more you know about your readers, the more precise you can make your writing. You have more certainty about what to say and how to say it. You're writing to people who are individuals. Of course, you may decide that an accountant is only an accountant and write to him or her on that basis. But it's a one-dimensional approach that makes life harder than it needs to be. You'll make sure that any financial information is clear and accurate, but the rest of your writing may feel flat and lose his or her attention. That's no fun for you *or* your accountant.

But what if I'm writing to a group of people who read every newspaper from *The Sun* to *The Financial Times*? Surely that's harder?

You're over sweating this point. You're not trying to replicate a style. These answers give you clues, but keep your perspective on what's important. Structure. Cutting jargon. Language choices. No one who reads either *The Sun* or *The Financial Times* objects to writing that's tight, a fast read, and easy to understand. The FT is no academic journal to start with. *The Sun* and the FT are both well written and easy to read.

But if my writing is a reflection of me, why do I have to think so heavily about my readers?

Your writing *is* a reflection of you, but you're confused about what this means. If you think only of *your* purpose, *your* needs, and *your* knowledge, why are you writing to anyone else? You'll come across as a self-centred egotist and no one will listen to you. When you think of writing as a two-way activity, you'll come across as a writer who thinks carefully about what others want to know, what's in it for them, and how to engage them. You'll be a writer people want to hear from.

Surely how I use my words is about my writing style, not about my readers?

You wouldn't word an invitation to a casual party in the same tone you'd use for an invitation to a formal AGM. How we dress and speak shows different moods and parts of our personality; we adapt to the occasion while still being ourselves. It's the same with writing. Even with your readers' needs front and centre, the authentic you can still shine through in your writing.

Isn't this making my writing manipulative?

Only if you believe *manipulative* to mean *smart*. When you imagine a picture of your readers, you'll recognise areas they'll welcome and others that worry them. You're not trying to trick them by leaving out information they might resist. At least, I hope that's not the case. Knowing about awkward areas that concern readers means you can tackle them head-on in a direct, way that inspires confidence. Of course, if you don't know enough about your readers to realise they have concerns... I'd call that dumb.

GAINING A CONNECTION.

Think of people you regularly write for.

What would they do with their lives if they didn't have to earn money?

_____

_____

_____

Can you name their favourite TV programme?

_____

_____

_____

Can you pinpoint an item on their bucket list?

_____

_____

_____

How often do you genuinely think of their needs while writing?

_____

_____

_____

'If a writer of prose knows enough about what he is writing about, he may omit things that he knows and the reader, if the writer is writing truly enough, will have a feeling of those things as strongly as though the writer had stated them. The dignity of movement of an iceberg is due to only one-eighth of it being above water.'

ERNEST HEMINGWAY

CHAPTER SEVEN
Icebergs ahead!

I admit being a research junkie. I'm also a cynic when people say they know enough about a subject to write 1,000, 2,000 or sometimes 40,000 words. Often they don't. When writers believe they know enough to start writing, what they're sometimes saying is they can include everything they know.

That's not nearly enough. These results will feel thin and stretched, lacking quality and depth. My work as a sub-editor on newspapers and magazines, and as a business writing mentor, has shown me many instances where writers stopped research too soon. Nervousness and insecurity oozes through their words.

When lack of space or shortage of reading time pushes you to leave out tons of information, magic shows up. Your writing becomes tighter and carries more impact because of the need to cram in as much value as possible while keeping your work short.

Gathering a mix of information and views pushes you deeper into the understanding of your subject. The ideas and achievements of others stimulate new thoughts of your own.

But a build-up of gravitas is the real magic. The writing you share becomes the tip of an iceberg, nine-tenths of it hidden. Readers recognise the weight of knowledge they can't see. What you cut shows between the lines; what you include stands on the shoulders of everything you cut.

When you produce great writing, you typically spend most of your time researching and accumulating knowledge that prompts new ideas to bubble up. Then you decide to leave most of it out. The research feels likely to be a complete waste.

And yet it works... because you made a conscious *decision* on what to include based on careful *thought*.

WHY GOING OFF-PISTE IS A GOOD THING

Tunnel vision works against creativity, particularly where research is concerned. Pursuing obvious routes justifies and reinforces what you know. It stops new ideas and insights forming.

What we know changes as our understanding of our world expands, and limiting your research can trip you up. *QI*, the popular quiz show hosted on British TV by national treasure Stephen Fry, captures its audience in a comical way with a quiz that highlights facts and figures that seem bizarre, fascinating and often unbelievable — until Fry reveals them to be credible. Yet within a year of any episode, seven per cent of what has been declared to be true will be incorrect, having been overtaken by new knowledge. Relying on what you know can be a mistake.

How do you know if drifting off the beaten track will be helpful or not — unless you go there?

Imagine yourself involved in the takeover of a prestigious, boutique fragrance house. You crunch company finances and compare the portfolio of fragrances with the rest of the market. Useful, but predictable.

If you go off-piste about the potential direction in which the company might go, you may wander into the industry's background and origins. You talk with perfumers about their craft, discovering how our sense of smell works.

You hear stories about how famous fragrances were born and marketed, and how they reflected the times from which they emerged. You discover *QI*-like information about the industry...

- We are born with no knowledge of odour, only 100 million olfactory nerve endings that learn to recognise smells and associate them with specific experiences. By our early teens, most of our smell 'fingerprint' is formed. Smell is the only sense we can't edit. Once it is embedded in our memory, we're stuck with that association.

- Guerlain's fragrance Shalimar was created to echo the story of Shah Jahan the last Mogul ruler of India, and his marriage to Mumtaz Mahal, the woman to whom he lost his heart. Jahan commissioned a garden made as a series of crystal pools and fountains, calling it Shalimar. The gardens were the couple's private place, where they would make love under the stars. Jahan was desperate for a son and heir, and Mahal became pregnant, although she wanted no more children. Mahal died giving birth to Jahan's longed-for son. Consumed by grief, Jahan commissioned artists and craftsmen to create a shrine in her memory, a shrine which took 13 years to finish and which stands today as the Taj Mahal.

- The Romans scented everything, even the mortar that made up their homes. When the sun shone, the fabric of the buildings became an orgy of fragrance.

- Natural civet — a fragrance component with a foul smell until mixed with other ingredients — has been replaced by a synthetic version. Traditionally, this waxy paste was spooned from a gland near the civet cat's anus — a painful process. The cats were caged and these cages banged to make the cats angry. The angrier they became, the more paste the cats produced.

- In 1946, Carven's Ma Griffe fragrance rained down on the post-war world in an innovative way. Tiny bottles of the fragrance were jettisoned over central Paris, each bottle attached to a tiny green-and-white parachute. A celebration of pilots trying to save lives, this gift symbolised the new post-war world. Paris came to a standstill as marketing came of age.

- Cleopatra used so much scent on the sails of her barges, it was said her approach could be detected miles downstream.

- One of the most costly of raw perfume materials is ambergris. It comes from the cachalot or sperm whale and forms when the whale swallows cuttlefish, whose bony beaks irritate the respiratory tract and intestine; the whale secretes a waxy paste around it as protection against irritation — much like a pearl forms inside an oyster. When it reaches a certain size, the whale expels it much like a cat expels a fur ball and it hardens as it bobs along the water. The largest piece found weighed 300 kilograms.

- When perfumer Henri Almeras created the fragrance Joy for the difficult-to-please couturier Jean Patou in 1929, Almeras never thought Patou would choose it. Almeras declared it impossible to create Joy as a commercial product as it had more concentrated raw materials than almost any other scent. 'Nonsense,' said Patou. 'Double the amount of "jus". It will be to perfume what Rolls Royce is to motor cars.'

  Wall Street crashed just before Joy was to be launched. Patou's business was hit hard as most of his clients were Americans who had become penniless overnight. Instead of shelving the project, Patou commissioned exclusive glass designer Baccarat to create a bottle and sent liveried footmen to deliver Joy to his wealthy clients.

This is a fraction of what you might discover. At worst, this diversion will give you a feel for an industry driven by passion. At best it will generate fresh, creative ideas. Some will be useful, some will seem crazy. All will deserve attention.

You may wonder, with good reason, what possessed someone to discover if the civet cat harboured a useful fragrance ingredient. Or why someone felt the urge to put whale vomit into a perfume. I can't say I'd blame you. But they demonstrate the value of going off-piste.

We have discovered that the Romans' fragranced mortar was ahead of the modern household fragrance plug-in. Maybe that knowledge was behind the plug-in's creation? We've discovered that Cleopatra could never creep up on anyone. And we've discovered that old stories may be able to show us the way toward creative product launches.

One more thing...

'A woman's perfume tells more about her than her handwriting.'

Christian Dior

Had Dior never heard of forensic linguistics?

HORROR STORY #8 – R FOR REMEDIAL

In 2012, The Confederation of British Industry reported that six per cent of businesses had to offer classes in literacy to university graduates.

A year earlier, CBI research showed that 42 per cent of employers weren't satisfied with the basic reading and writing skills of school and college leavers: almost half had to invest in remedial training.

Yet, more than 90 per cent of career professionals cite the 'need to write effectively' as a 'skill of great importance' in their daily work.

HOW RESEARCH CAN OPEN DOORS

Good writing solves problems, as you gather and analyse information in search of creative answers. Allow yourself to go off-piste and you may come up with something that will save time and grief.

Two independent producers warmed to a contemporary film script of mine, and we joined forces to raise the $15m budget, a considerable sum, but low for a mainstream film. They suggested the need for an A-list acting lead as safety for investors' money. Big names don't always guarantee success, but they are a comforting place to start.

We pursued this approach and drew a great response —yet we stalled.

I researched films in the same genre, going back as far as 20 years, looking at how they were made and their routes to success. Some had A-list stars; some didn't. Some had large budgets; some were shot on a shoestring. Some opened in a small number of cinemas and built audiences on good word of mouth, taking as long as a year to finish their trawl through cinemas. Some opened everywhere at once, on a large publicity spend and disappeared fast. Yet all were successful.

On the surface, the only shared thread seemed to be luck.

With further research, a pattern emerged. The A-list presence was always there — but not always in front of the camera. Studio backing, a famous producer, clever distribution and marketing. These all brought much needed clout.

The answer was clear: look beyond the A-list actor to an A-list producer, director or distributor. Our options opened up, the project became unstuck, and we're working on it now...

Think yourself into an investor's shoes. Isn't this the kind of problem-solving homework you'd want to see?

ASKING THE RIGHT QUESTIONS

Common journalism wisdom says there are only six questions you can ask: *who, what, where, when, why* and *how*? And yet, as part of my book research, I discovered the European Union includes a seventh question — *how much*? — in its writing guidelines.

Each question has many levels with increasing depth to the answers. It's up to you to decide how far you want to take your research.

Questions challenge your thinking and the deeper you go, the chances increase that you'll change your mind about what you think. You'll go beyond the superficial, and sometimes abandon allegiance to beliefs you previously held to be sound. Risk uncovering new thoughts and insights and you risk discovering your old thinking to be deluded or misguided.

It may be scary, but an enquiring mind helps you to avoid potential mistakes in judgment, pushing you towards clearer thinking.

DON'T FORGET A HIDDEN RESOURCE

You started asking questions as soon as you learned to think. We are a species that insists on trying to make sense of what we see and experience. We try to work out *why* someone behaves in a certain way, *what* prompts a company to change course and *how* they make it work, *what* makes people change their voting habits and elect a new government, *who* will be our next prime minister, *where* the next big idea will come from, or *when* is a good time to propose marriage.

We test and process new information against everything we already believe to be true. The answers we accumulate to our relentless questions — whether or not they're based on solid reasoning — build into a database we can draw on. We just need to watch for the signs of it trying to pop out and show us something.

Since you are the only one with your set of experiences, your database is unique; it's the reason you will never write anything in exactly the same way as anyone else. You have little choice but to be you — unless you suppress your instincts. If you fail to use this talent, your contribution to the world will be lost.

But remember: readers have instincts too. They can sniff out something that's misguided, or that relies on thinking that's dated.

Resting on your laurels where your existing knowledge is strong can be a pitfall. Where films are concerned — one of my passions in life

— I may become complacent when I feel I have little to learn. *Dances with Wolves* may easily become *Dancing with Wolves* when I forget I don't know everything.

Yet my maths weakness becomes a strength when I see the need for diligence. As a journalist covering company finances, I was once able to point out to the finance director of a public limited company that his accounts were wrong. It was a simple typo with two numbers in the wrong place. Yet I was right and his team of experienced accountants was wrong.

Even so, my friends never ask me to divide a restaurant bill of £1,000, including service, between ten people. My version will involve fractions... or quadratic equations I don't understand.

HORROR STORY #9 – SINGLE SPELLING SLIP STOPS SALES!

Webshop entrepreneur Charles Duncombe wondered why one of his sites was underperforming. Correcting a single typo on the site doubled sales overnight. 'You get about six seconds to capture someone's attention on a website. Cutting edge companies depend on old-fashioned skills,' he says. 'When you sell or communicate on the internet, 99 per cent of the time it is done by the written word.'

THE UPSIDE OF RESEARCH

Extensive research means you'll never have to say: 'I'm sorry, I didn't know that'. Research gets people hooked on you and what you know. They buy into you as a hard worker, someone with an open mind and commitment to a job well done.

People like to hang around people who know things. Even better, they want to do business with people who are curious and who find answers; an enquiring mind is a magnetic quality. Some of your knowledge may, like the civet cat and whale vomit instances, show you going off-piste, but they're never dull and show you as thorough. You're not afraid to explore dead ends because you know they're never a waste of time.

The deeper you go with research, the more the amount of knowledge you discover forces you to decide what to include and what to leave out. Often these are tough choices. Readers become the core of your filtering system and you learn to test everything against what they need to know. You cut anything that fails this test.

Your reader filter pushes you to anticipate questions they may ask; everything you're holding back adds to the confidence you take with you to follow-up meetings. People see you as an authority and take your views seriously.

You haven't written a word, yet you're becoming a writer whose work is worth reading.

'Get your facts first, and then you can distort them as much as you please.'

MARK TWAIN

FAQs

Where do I find the time to do all this research?

Can you afford to do otherwise? I'm sure you don't want superficial results. I'm guessing you normally spend about 20 per cent of your writing time on research, planning and working out what your readers need — and the remaining 80 per cent putting words together and becoming frustrated because the results are never as good as you want them to be. This is a back-to-front approach, one that makes your writing thinner. You will spend more time rewriting. If you spend the bulk of your time on purpose, your readers, research and planning, the words flow more easily in the time you have left. Shift how you allocate your time in small steps and you'll acclimatise to what feels, at first, like a risky approach.

Doing lots of research and then leaving it out seems a waste of time. What's the point?

The point is to bring gravitas to your work, enabling you to write with authority. You can only do that if you know more than you're using. There are no shortcuts to great writing. Who wants to be seen as a lightweight thinker?

Is there such a thing as too much research?
If you run out of time and don't get your writing finished — yes. Pace yourself.

I'm confused. Where do my instincts come in?
Instincts are the barometer you use to test your ideas and proposals. All of your experiences are randomly stored in your head; nothing is filed and organised. Your instincts try to make sense of these random thoughts, experiences and knowledge. They tell you if your judgment is on track or misguided. Of course, if you put rubbish into your head, some of your instincts will be based on rubbish.

WHEN ENOUGH IS NOT ALWAYS ENOUGH

How much of your time do you spend on research before writing?

_____

_____

_____

When you write, do you pack in everything you know?

_____

_____

_____

While writing, do you ever realise you don't know enough?

_____

_____

_____

How can you improve your approach?

_____

_____

_____

'Without an outline, you're going to write yourself all over the page — and sometimes, off it.'

MELANIE BLUE

CHAPTER EIGHT
Template? What template?

ANYONE who's tried meditating knows how randomly our minds work, and how hard it is to control our thoughts. *At last, my mind is empty... how long has it been?... what shall I eat tonight?... I must empty my mind... wow, this is hard... oh no, I'm still thinking... is it possible to meditate more quickly?* Our focus wanders off on its own journey.

Similar frustrations occur when we write without a plan in place. Irrelevant thoughts pop up, worries about whether you've missed gathering information, anxiety about what your readers might want, insecurities about the chance of ending up with a mess.

Few people love outlines. But the horrid truth is that while they feel like the devil's invention, having an outline saves time and makes our writing more coherent.

For a five-paragraph email, you may want as little as five words to prompt what each paragraph should be about. *Summary. Costs. Timetable. Pitfalls. Suggestions.* With a handful of words, a plan you may be able to hold in your head without writing it down, you'll roll out information in a sensible order. When you've finished the draft email, you may decide that *costs* have become the most urgent area you want readers to focus on. An easy fix. Five paragraphs are easy to reshuffle before you send your email.

Longer documents, made up of sections, sidebars and appendices, need a more considered plan. Wing your way through a long document with no outline and you have a more than average chance of producing a mess that demands more extensive editing than it might otherwise have needed. Follow an outline and you start editing from a better place.

You can never have too much clarity. Coherent structure is the sign of an organised mind and it gives readers the confidence to follow you. People who know where they're going attract followers. People who stop and wonder which path to take end up following someone with a map.

Clarity keeps people reading because you deliver information at the right time — usually when a question pops into a reader's mind — a little like laying a trail of breadcrumbs. You avoid asking readers to wade through diversions, wondering if you intend to get back to the point. And well-structured writing is not just quicker to read, it stays in readers' minds for longer.

> ### HORROR STORY #10 – DON'T MAKE HYPHENS A TOP SECRET
>
> A nuclear plant supervisor ordered 'ten foot long lengths' of radioactive material. Instead of getting the ten-foot lengths it needed and thought would arrive, the plant received ten one-foot lengths, a mistake with a cost so great the information was classified.

HEADING OFF PROBLEMS

When you plan your structure, you increase the chance of spotting flaws before you start writing and become attached to your words. Early fixes save time, frustration — and money. Writing may be a by-product of your main job, but you're still paid to write, albeit in an indirect way. You owe it to whoever pays your salary — even if that's you — to be as professional as possible. Fail to plan and you'll be stuck with C- writing.

Unless you're a professional writer — someone who gets paid for words as an end in themselves — you probably have a nervous school legacy about your language skills. Memories of red pen scrawls berating your grammar, punctuation or spelling may haunt you. Planning helps you to raise this part of your game.

With a plan as your guide, you no longer have to worry about where you're going. You can concentrate on how to express your thoughts and relax into writing well.

Spontaneous thoughts will pop up as you write and that's great. In fact, they're more likely to appear when you approach writing as a process. You've cleared your mind and allowed space for fresh insights to appear. You can drop these into your draft, if they are small and easy to handle. If they constitute a big idea, demanding extra research and, perhaps, the creation of a new section, make a note to include them when you've finished your draft.

Despite your best efforts, you will still write some rubbish, so get used to the idea that rewriting is mandatory. But you face less of it if you write with careful thought and with a plan at your side.

SO WHERE'S THE TEMPLATE?

Many books offer blueprints on how to write the perfect email, sales pitch, CV, mission statement, investment proposals and other specific documents. This is not one of these books.

Offering you ways to avoid making important structural choices is a cheat. There is no shortcut, or magic bullet, that offers you a chance to avoid thinking — not if you're aiming for great writing. When you do your own thinking, you don't need templates.

What you write, and how you structure your writing, is a reflection of *your* aims, *your* readers' needs, *your* content — and, sometimes, legal niceties that have to be included in specific documents. Investment outlines, for instance, have to comply with conditions that allow you to attract funding without turning it into a crime. It would be dumb to ignore these in the interests of being original; you'll find yourself in trouble. But you need a lawyer or accountant to advise on these kinds of issues. A template isn't the answer.

When you are free from legal necessities, you have the chance for creative thought that can filter into your structure, something you won't achieve by following someone else's ideas. You can't nudge the world when you're in a straitjacket. Likewise, you're unlikely to achieve much if you're rebelling for the sake of it.

Be guided by your purpose and your readers' needs. Mission statements need to nail a company's ambitions and culture while inspiring others to jump on board. Strategy documents need to show which way to go and why. Pitch documents need to persuade others to award a contract, offer funding or join a project. Emails need to cover a host of aims.

You don't need a blueprint; you need a way to assemble your thoughts and it's up to you to decide what suits you best. It's what you signed up for when you decided you'd like to nudge the world a little.

Some people like visual mind maps as a way of exploring and arranging their thoughts. I hate them. I prefer written outlines, sometimes locking down minute detail. At other times, a handful of cryptic words is enough to guide me. Find a way that suits you.

Don't let the word 'outline' intimidate you. There's no need for something formal that wins anyone else's approval; your outline doesn't have to make sense to anyone but you.

No one is going to mark your outline.

LEARN FROM THE PROS

The work of professional writers offers clues on how to structure in a subtle way that helps gain and hold readers' attention. Take a look at a major issue covered in the news and see how different newspapers and magazines structure their coverage.

Coverage of the country's annual budget announcement is a great example. Tabloid titles will have short sections that cover the *who, what, where, why* and *how* of the subject in bite-sized chunks. They'll make a big deal of what most concerns their readers and make less of, or even ignore, elements their readers don't care about. Some sections may use a question-and-answer approach. Charts, graphics, bullet points, and sidebars may support a main article that gives the big picture. If you try this with a selection of newspapers, remember you're looking at structural choices, not language style.

Newspapers we describe as the quality press often take a different approach with fewer sections and less emphasis on visual pyrotechnics. Each newspaper tackles the same story in a distinctive way, guided by their readership's wants and needs.

You may be tackling a subject that splits into readymade sections. If you hope to win a contract, you're likely to want team biographies to boost credibility and confidence. You may have an FAQ section to sweep up issues that are most easily dealt with in this way. You may have areas where you can offer bullet points that get information across quickly and with impact. You'll have a timetable or schedule, targets, an overview giving a quick snapshot of the essentials, and much more. Deciding the priorities of these sections is your choice and depends on context.

You may also want to structure your document so that distinct sections take on a life of their own and can be sent to specific readers with only limited interest in the rest of your material. Or you may decide on a structure that easily allows people to skip over areas that aren't crucial to them. Potential investors, for instance, may jump straight to the commercial potential and number crunching areas, coming back to general sections later. Think, plan and explore...

CREATING WAVES

Split long documents into sections and you give yourself the chance to renew readers' commitment as they start each one. Sections offer you the chance to establish a rhythm to your writing. None of us wants to read something that hits the same note on every page. We want variety.

Try grabbing readers' attention with an inverted pyramid structure to each of your sections — see the illustration below.

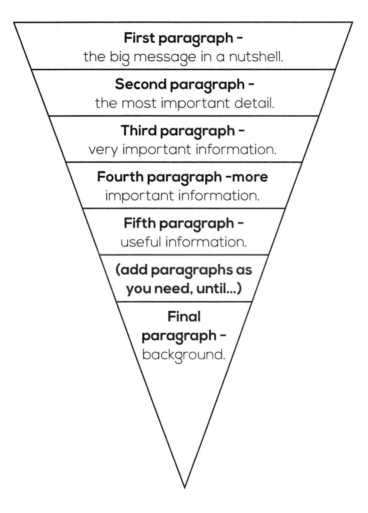

First paragraph -
the big message in a nutshell.

Second paragraph -
the most important detail.

Third paragraph -
very important information.

Fourth paragraph -more
important information.

Fifth paragraph -
useful information.

(add paragraphs as
you need, until...)

Final
paragraph -
background.

The first paragraph is the one you want people to read if they have only 60 seconds before they catch a long-haul flight. If you write this paragraph well enough, they'll take your document on their journey. This is the ultimate précis of what you want to say — either in a section, or the entire document — without going into detail. Ideally, this should be fewer than 50 words. If you feel this is impossible to write, your thinking is muddled and you need to clarify exactly what you want to say.

After this, everything you need to trickle out to your readers is rolled out in descending order of importance. The number of paragraphs in the illustration is an example only; use as many paragraphs as you need, as long as you keep a hold on how much readers need to hear and how much you should ask of their time.

At the end, you have the opportunity to tuck in background. If background is context that readers must have to avoid being puzzled before they read on, try to slip it in as an aside. Or turn it into your second paragraph. Keep it brief, or you'll bore readers by telling them something that isn't your main objective.

You may feel that front loading information stops people reading further on the grounds that one paragraph says everything. It doesn't and they won't — not if you do it well. This approach grabs attention and challenges your readers to give up, knowing they're already hooked.

Even better, you get to deliver this punch with each section.

Let's have a look at a two-paragraph example from an investment story based on a British Film Institute report that proclaimed British film as a growing global brand.

The breakout success of *The King's Speech* and *The Inbetweeners* helped independent British film to a strong 2011.

These two films alone accounted for 13.5 per cent of the $1.4bn spent at the UK box office in that year, according to figures from the British Film Institute.

The first paragraph gives a concise version of the big picture without getting bogged down in detail. The next paragraph backs up the first paragraph with the nuts and bolts that support the statement already made.

Yet we want to know more... and if we decide we've had enough, we can skip to the next section. Readers are busy. Help them to get to the parts that most interest them.

And you can apply the inverted pyramid structure for an entire document... each section... paragraph... even to individual sentences.

'A blank piece of paper is God's way of telling us how hard it is to be God.'

SIDNEY SHELDON

FAQs

I'm sure I've read about authors who take a more spontaneous approach. Do I really have to plan when professional writers don't?

These authors are often writing the kind of literary fiction where character exploration, not plot, is the aim. Don't forget they are making everything up. You're not. While some novelists may free fall, journalists know where they're going before they write. Experience trains them on how to hold a structure in their head. But they still have a plan...

Do I have to? Even with a short email?

You can bounce through structural decisions in your head for short emails. But you're still making choices. If you have one word for each paragraph in your head, then you have a plan.

What if my bosses insist that I stick to a particular format?

Try to convince them to allow a more creative approach. If they insist, aim for something fresh within the restrictions you have. If you feel strongly enough, you might want to produce two documents, one of them taking a more creative approach. See which your bosses choose, while being prepared for them to be less adventurous than you. This is about long-term purpose, not short-term wins.

I'm slightly freaked out by the inverted pyramid approach. Aren't my readers going to get bored if my writing keeps tailing off?

Using the inverted pyramid doesn't mean your writing has to tail away. Recognise when you've done the job, and have the confidence to stop.

But I'd really like a 'wow' finish. Can't I save some really important info until the end?

Please don't. Your readers probably won't get to it. You'll have puzzled them to the point where they stop reading. Don't try to manipulate readers. Focus on engaging them with your knowledge and insight. You aren't writing a mystery novel, saving the big reveal to the end.

What about saving some really important information for a meeting? Is that better?

No. That's a recipe for disaster. You seem to imagine you won't have anything to discuss because you've written too well. If you can't write well enough, what makes you think you'll get a meeting? Your writing is a conversation in its own right and can sometimes make a meeting redundant. Don't let this freak you out. Would you prefer a pointless meeting or an email that says: '*Well done. Go ahead, and keep me posted.*'?

But what about my leftover research? When do I use it?

You're still using it, even when it's not in your writing. It gives your writing gravitas and forces tight writing. And when you get to a meeting, you'll be the expert with even more knowledge to share, demonstrating that you've done way more homework than anyone realised.

FAIL TO PLAN?

Do you always prepare an outline, even a rough one, before you write?

_____

_____

_____

_____

_____

_____

_____

Do you have a method that works for you? Mind maps? Notes?

_____

_____

_____

_____

_____

_____

_____

Do you normally stick to a template or blueprint?
Does this work for you or limit you?

_____

_____

_____

_____

_____

Do you microstructure within sections?

_____

_____

_____

_____

_____

Where could you do better?

_____

_____

_____

_____

_____

_____

PART THREE

Words, words, words...

'The first draft of anything is shit.'

ERNEST HEMINGWAY

'Writing is easy. All you have to do is cross out the wrong words.'

MARK TWAIN

'When people tell you something's wrong, or doesn't work for them, they are almost always right. When they tell you exactly what they think is wrong and how to fix it, they are almost always wrong.'

NEIL GAIMAN

'I don't think writers are sacred, but words are. They deserve respect. If you get the right ones in the right order, you might nudge the world a little...'

TOM STOPPARD

CHAPTER NINE
Are you active or Zzzzzzz?

MANY business writers want readers to see them as dynamic and active, and then produce work that shows them as passive and indirect — all without realising what they've done.

> **Carol <u>wrote</u> the business proposal.** *(active)*
>
> **The business proposal was <u>written</u> by Carol.** *(passive)*
>
> **The business proposal was <u>written</u>.** *(passive)*

These examples show the difference between the active and passive voices, the only two we use in our writing. The first sentence shows Carol being active and taking action — writing her business proposal, and maybe hoping for a pay rise or promotion. The second focuses on the business proposal being written, and the third shows how we can lose what may be vital information by ditching Carol completely. So much for any hopes of a pay rise.

When we use the active voice, we show a *doer* acting on an *object*. In our active example, Carol is the doer, writing is her action, and the business proposal is the object she acts on. We've created a sentence that's quick and easy to understand.

But when we choose the passive voice, we put the doer after the verb and end up with a flat sentence that uses more words — while losing energy.

Active writing carries more impact. Most of what we read in newspapers and magazines is active; it's the kind of writing we pay to read and newspapers need to sell what they write. It's also how we prefer to speak.

Passive writing often feels evasive, as if the writer is trying to get off the hook for action we may find objectionable. Where it enables us to drop any mention of the 'doer' it may feel like confirmation that we're trying to dodge a bullet. Do I need to point out that it makes us sound... passive?

So why is the passive voice common in business writing? It feels detached and formal, and implies objectivity that's often an illusion. It often makes writing feel boring and obscure, yet we cling to this approach on the grounds that it sounds more professional and carries added authority. It doesn't.

The point is not to avoid passive sentences completely since there are circumstances when they are useful. We should aim to make a conscious choice based on what we want to achieve.

Let's look at some further examples.

Mary threw Bob out of the house last night. *(active)*

Bob was thrown out of the house last night by Mary. *(passive)*

We're more likely to opt for the active version here, whether or not we feel Mary was being reasonable. She's the one taking action; that's what grabs our attention and makes the sentence lively.

Of course, Bob may take action next and we're likely to move our focus to what he does.

Bob threw his keys at an upstairs window. *(active)*

The upstairs window was hit by Bob's keys. *(passive)*

Of course, active sentences don't have to involve people at all, nor does the action have to be the kind you'd find in a Hollywood action film.

Leaves covered the ground. *(active)*

The ground was covered with leaves. *(passive)*

The choice here is less obvious and you might choose either version, depending on the context and how poetic you choose to be.

Blood covered the body. *(active)*

The body was covered with blood. *(passive)*

In this example, I'd choose the passive version because I'm more interested in the body: the passive sentence carries a more dramatic punch. I can feel the implied emphasis on the word *covered*. But would a forensic scientist writing to police investigators choose differently? Maybe.

Where your building works are concerned, several mistakes have been admitted. *(passive)*

This is an ugly sentence and sounds evasive since no one owns the mistakes. Readers want answers and may zoom in on areas where omissions seem part of a cover-up.

Don't forget that you want each of your readers to arrive at the same meaning, despite bringing different experiences to their reading. If the building works in this sentence took place at a block of flats with dozens of residents, they may each attribute the mistakes to different people — workmen, the site foreman, or the building company. They may even feel that they are being implicated in the mistakes.

It makes more sense to be direct.

Where your building works are concerned, we/I admit making several mistakes. *(active)*

This version is better since someone owns up. But it's still ugly.

We/I admit making several mistakes in carrying out your building works. *(active)*

This no-nonsense version is active, direct and unlikely to inflame readers — unless, of course, the mistakes aren't fixed.

A well-meant desire to avoid finger pointing may come back to bite you in surprising ways.

A member of the accounts department was accused of fraud. *(passive)*

If the accounts department has a small enough staff, one of them may feel relieved by the anonymity, but the rest may feel rightly aggrieved on the grounds that colleagues believe them to be crooks.

None of us wants to make accusations, but it's generally best to tell the truth and take a direct approach to expressing it. Do we need an active version of this example? Maybe.

Legal issues may stop us from naming someone. This sounds safe until you realise that the innocent members of staff may all be able to sue for defamation of character. Even without being named, a small enough group may be able to demonstrate that colleagues believe suspicion has fallen on them.

When you write in an authentic way, a direct approach is generally best. Directness may upset someone, but when you are aware of the possibility and take pains to be precise, accurate and fair, you will be confident enough to stand by your words. At worst, you want to narrow down the number of people you anger.

There are circumstances where knowing who took action is implied or irrelevant. Journalists are skilled at making passive sentences powerful and dynamic, particularly when legal issues restrict how much can be said.

Police today arrested a 35-year-old man for the murder of... *(active)*

A 35-year-old man was arrested today for the murder of... *(passive)*

Here, we are more interested in who has been arrested than we are in who made the arrest — we understand that this is usually the police. Stories of this type would be boring if they all took the same active voice approach.

Breaking into a sweat over a single misplaced passive sentence may seem a little obsessive. But it sometimes takes only one poorly constructed sentence to upset readers. A document riddled with passive sentences will drive readers away, or entice them to pick up a loaded gun.

Microsoft Word and analytic software highlight passive sentences with good reason. The active voice is easier to read than the passive one. It's that simple.

It may take time to diagnose if you have a passive sentence habit and you may find it hard to recognise the clues. Word and Hemingway flag up possible passive sentences in your work. Or you can search for them yourself, if you prefer.

Find the word *was* in your verb and you may be looking at a passive sentence. It's not an infallible guide — and the building works example I've used in this chapter is a variation that brings in *have been.*

The business proposal <u>was</u> written by Carol.

The business proposal <u>was</u> written.

Bob <u>was</u> thrown out of the house last night by Mary.

The upstairs window <u>was</u> hit by Bob's keys.

The ground <u>was</u> covered with leaves.

The body <u>was</u> covered with blood.

A member of the accounts department <u>was</u> accused of fraud.

A 35-year-old man <u>was</u> arrested today for the murder of...

Where your building works are concerned, several mistakes <u>have been</u> admitted.

Passive writing as a comfortable habit leads to poor writing. In business writing, it's the hardest habit to change, mostly because it's an ingrained and unconscious choice.

Persevere and you will infuse your writing with life and energy.

'A man's grammar, like Caesar's wife, should not only be pure, but above suspicion of impurity.'

EDGAR ALLAN POE

FAQs

The active voice seems too blunt. Are you sure I'm not better off with something gentler?

When you cling to passive writing, ask yourself why. There are no trick questions here and changing circumstances will produce opposite choices. Are you afraid to be direct and upfront? Or is passive a good choice? Feathers may need to be ruffled for a good reason. It depends on the context, your writing goals, and your readers.

You are making roughly the same point, even if you choose the passive voice. So if you can't bring yourself to write actively, should you say it at all? Does it feel honest or mildly sneaky? Only you can make this choice. Do it consciously.

Of course, if you have a heavy passive sentence habit, your readers may be giving up on you long before you have a chance to upset them. Or they may be zoned out, glossing over your meaning and not really taking it in.

But I feel as if I'm accusing people when they've made simple mistakes. Isn't this a legitimate use of the passive voice?
It may be. I'm not suggesting that you behave like a bully or an internet troll. You should aim to be fair, accurate and reasonable all of the time, not only when the active/passive choice occurs. If someone has made a mistake, it's a chance to tackle a problem head-on. Or is there an upside to being indirect? Challenge yourself before deciding what kind of voice to use. Choose your words carefully and aim for balance.

Doesn't active writing seem angry and abrupt?
Not if you choose words with care. Direct is different from angry. You won't please everyone — however you write — and it's unreasonable to expect otherwise. What do people think of your existing work? Evasive? Inconclusive? Wishy-washy? Try to take a balanced view. I'm not suggesting that you banish passive sentences since they sometimes serve a purpose.

Is there a passive sentence limit I should stick to?

No. Context should be your guide. We're individuals with different quirks and preferences; with practice and analysis of your own style, you'll build up a history that lets you know what feels right for you. I've come across people with a passive writing habit of 80+ per cent. They usually have a certain kind of professional training: scientists, academics, doctors, lawyers or accountants. And they're usually unaware of their habit. When they realise what they're doing, they often shift to something more reader-friendly.

If I use more active sentences, do I really become a more active person?

Yes, if you're comfortable doing it. Writing is a reflection of who you are. Don't force this: that's when it doesn't work. You have to feel comfortable with your writing. As a general rule, you are what you write. So if writing more actively feels good, you will be acting in the same way.

'The main rule of writing is that if you do it with enough assurance and confidence you're allowed to do whatever you like.'

NEIL GAIMAN

CHAPTER TEN

Being positive – even if you're sad

ANYONE who has tried to lose weight or stop smoking knows that focusing on avoiding a habit often reinforces it. Our brains don't hear 'lose weight' or 'stop smoking': they hear 'weight' and 'smoking' and we end up with more of what we're trying to get rid of.

When we write something as a negative expression — often using words with 'un-', 'not' and similar negative add-ons — our brains have to think of the positive and cancel it before we can grasp the meaning. Our writing becomes slow and hard to read.

So why not cut straight to a positive expression, even when we're describing a negative action?

He does not play fairly. *(negative)*

He cheats. *(positive)*

The positive version — and *he cheats* is a positive expression of a negative action — is direct and may feel a step too far to some writers. Yet both versions make the accusation, the negative form taking a passive-aggressive approach. Is that who you are? Why not be upfront? Or consider if you should say it at all.

Jane is often not on time. *(negative)*

Jane is often late. *(positive)*

Jane often works late. *(positive)*

I doubt that Jane would object to being described as a hard worker. As a result, writing this positive statement in Jane's annual appraisal probably feels like a no-brainer. But if you wince at making a similar statement about her timekeeping, then you're adjusting your writing style to dodge possible confrontation. Is that the real you?

You can use subtle graduations when using the positive form, using context as your touchstone.

The sales team did not meet its monthly sales target. *(negative)*

The sales team failed to meet its monthly sales target. *(positive)*

The sales team fell short of its monthly sales target. *(positive)*

The sales team missed its monthly sales target. *(positive)*

Each statement makes the same factual point. *Fail* is a strong verb and you may feel this to be too strong and, perhaps, unkind. *Fell short* and *missed* are positive expressions, but softer than *fail*. Ah, they *fell short*. Oh, they *missed* it. They'll probably do better next month...

Choosing a direct, positive expression to describe negative results should prompt the question: why didn't they hit the target? Deal with this on the spot, with the question hanging in readers' minds, and you've tackled an issue, instead of trying to hide a statement that will feel like an accusation to the sales team, no matter how you say it.

Had the team hit the sales target, would they have felt aggrieved if you wrote ... *exceeded* its sales target... *beat* its sales target... *surpassed* its sales target? I doubt it. Choosing to use the negative form does not alter the underlying message; it just makes it slightly less obvious. It may also create ambiguity for readers, who may have less information or background knowledge than you.

Six athletes did not meet the drug testing criteria. *(negative)*

Six athletes failed a drugs test. *(positive)*

The negative version sounds evasive. Did the athletes miss their appointment? Did they forget to sign a form? If you aren't familiar with what's involved, you might be puzzled and uncertain.

The positive form is no-nonsense. Avoid embellishing the positive form with apologetic qualifying words and phrases such as '*Unfortunately, six athletes failed a drugs test...*' instead of sticking to what you know. Maybe this failure is a good thing?

Using the positive form does more than produce easy to read writing. It pushes you to define what you know.

The company ceased trading because of a lack of funds. *(negative)*

The company went into voluntary/ compulsory liquidation. *(positive)*

Here, the positive form encourages a forensic approach to choosing words, one that offers subtle distinction about whether or not the company was pushed or jumped into liquidation.

You probably know people who are *not rich* — a negative expression of a negative financial state. Are they *poor, destitute* or *solvent?* These are all positive expressions even though the financial positions vary. Being *not rich* leaves room for too much guesswork.

You may consider some people to be *not honest.* Are they *dishonest, deluded, corrupt, deceitful* or downright *fraudulent?* Some of these words should scare you — particularly since someone may take legal action if you use them. But do you imagine that *not honest* would get you off the hook? It won't.

Using the negative form brings one final pitfall that may make your head hurt — double negatives.

I see <u>no</u> reason why the sales team <u>should</u> <u>not</u> hit its sales target next month. *(double negative)*

It is reasonable to expect the sales team to meet its target next month. *(positive)*

Some people can take the negative form to brain frying limits...

He does <u>not</u> play fair, and I am <u>unconvinced</u> that the authorities will <u>not</u> view his behaviour as <u>ungentlemanly</u>. *(multi-negative)*

He cheats, and I am convinced the authorities will take a dim view of his behaviour. *(positive)*

Making a statement in a negative form often makes writing weak and non-committal — as well as baffling — while the positive form nails the meaning. Ultimately the choice is up to you. Just beware of staying in your comfort zone where you delude yourself that you are usefully fudging awkward issues.

The difference lies in being direct or defuse. Taking the direct route as often as possible will win respect for your straightforward approach; being indirect makes readers wary.

Playing it safe is often the most dangerous choice to make.

'Don't give people what they want, give them what they need.'

JOSS WHEDON

FAQs

None of these so-called positive examples sound positive to me. Am I missing something?

Using the positive form when writing is different from having a cheery, optimistic outlook on life where you only think positive thoughts. Neither does it mean writing only about nice things, lovely people and good news. It simply means choosing words that deliver your meaning directly — whether or not you have good or bad news.

What's the problem with a little softness?

It depends why you're making that choice. If you are trying to avoid confrontation, ask yourself why. If you're happy with your answer, stick with the soft approach. I'd suggest you avoid a soft, sometimes passive-aggressive approach as a comfortable habit. No one likes someone who always beats around the bush. We often have to show a tough, no-nonsense approach to difficult situations. We have different parts to our personality. Why not show them in your writing?

Doesn't this kind of writing nail me as a bully, someone who likes to throw accusations around?
No. It shows you to be someone who cuts to the heart of problems. Were you to expand on these examples, you could deliver some analysis and answers as well as making clear statements. Having the courage to use the positive form will often push your accuracy and balance. Using the negative form will often show you to be a people pleaser who ducks tough situations.

What if the positive form feels uncomfortable?
Then stick with the negative form until you're confident enough to do otherwise. It's your writing and your choice to change it or keep your existing approach. Take baby steps and see how small changes work. Your writing is a reflection of you and you're unlikely to go straight from a six-stone weakling to a heavyweight contender in one piece of writing.

'I never write metropolis for seven cents because I can get the same price for city. I never write policeman because I can get the same money for cop.'

MARK TWAIN

CHAPTER ELEVEN
What do you really mean?

WHEN we write, we paint pictures with words and we want everyone to see the same picture. We start by recognising that we each have different backgrounds, knowledge and viewpoints, depending on the experiences we bring to writing. Given these variations, the trick to clarity is simple: be specific.

A large pay rise means something different to a City banker than it does to a factory worker earning the minimum wage. A small drop in share price may concern a shareholder but spark only mild interest in a financial analyst. A tiny reduction in staff numbers sounds like a useful step to a company boss but may be a reason for a strike call for a union official.

As a journalist, I'm used to an industry where decisions are made and results produced by the end of the day. That's my idea of a 'reasonable timeframe'. To you, three months or three years might sound less alarming.

A big house... a major earthquake... huge change. All are open to a variety of meanings that leave writing ambiguous and puzzling. Vagueness implies you have forgotten your readers, their experiences and circumstances — along with the need to give them detail. Not only are you imposing *your* meaning onto their world, you're also not even telling your readers the rules of your world.

Vagueness invites confusion, may come across as misleading and, at worst, set off alarm bells about a lack of homework or honesty. Ultimately, vague writing signals your thinking to be... vague.

Being a research junkie saves you from a drift towards vague writing. A large building becomes 30 storeys with room for 20,000 office workers and parking spaces for 2,000 cars. A large pay rise becomes 50 per cent of basic pay with a bonus of three times our salary. A big house becomes a seven bedroom, six bathroom mansion with a double garage, a carriage driveway, indoor and outdoor heated swimming pools, stables for three horses, garaging for four cars, along with six acres of manicured grounds.

Specific, concrete words create impact and paint detailed pictures in readers' heads. They show you as a person capable of clear thinking based on solid knowledge, all of it showing up in vigorous, tight writing.

Weather forecasters predict a period of bad weather.

Weather forecasters predict ten inches of rain, hailstones the size of golf balls, and winds of more than 80 miles an hour for the next six days.

Don't leave anyone guessing about what you want them to see in their heads. You're not writing a mystery novel, remember. Even if you were, you'd use this level of detail.

KEEP IT SIMPLE

Lack of detail isn't always the main issue. Grandiose words, clichés and jargon are equally objectionable and likely to creep in if you have skimped on research. When people are trying to impress a reader with their intelligence, jargon is often the cheap trick they use. Mostly it demonstrates the opposite quality.

The first words we learned are the simple ones, the most familiar and usually the most effective. We asked our parents to *buy* us some chocolate, not to *purchase* it. We certainly didn't ask them to *acquire* it, which could carry a less savoury meaning in some contexts. Stick with simple words. They hit home quicker.

Jargon is tempting. But don't assume your readers are as familiar with it as you.

Business icon Richard Branson, a man you would hardly call an underachiever, has blogged about the need to avoid jargon. Branson has dyslexia, dropped out of school at the age of 16 and went on to experience various business ups and downs. His Virgin group holds more than 200 companies, including space tourism company Virgin Galactic.

In his blog, Branson admitted failing to know the difference between net and gross for many years, despite running several billion dollar companies.

'A few years ago, we were looking into investing money in a financial company,' he wrote. 'The person I was talking to said: "We only have a five per cent bid offer spread." Later, I asked one of my team what the guy was talking about. He explained they were using jargon as a way of hiding the fact they were stealing five per cent before we even started.'

Allow your thinking, not the length and obscurity of your words, to impress your readers. In one crucial aspect, writing is no different from any other craft or profession. Ask a perfumer what they are trying to create with a new fragrance and the answer will be 'simplicity'. An architect, an aircraft engineer, or a car designer will each make a similar statement. Simple is good. Complicated carries less impact.

Here are a handful of overly complicated words and phrases in daily use; some are relatively inoffensive on their own. But pepper these kinds of words throughout a long document and your readers will think you pompous.

ascertain	find out
as a consequence of	because
commence	begin, start
despatch	send
despite the fact that	although, despite
due to the fact that	as, because
endeavour	try
facilitate	help
for the duration of	during, while
in conjunction with	with
in order to	to
in the near future	soon
in the event of	if, when
particulars	details, facts
prior to	before
regarding	about
remuneration	pay, wages, salary
utilise	use
verify	check, prove
with reference to	about, concerning

On one of my training courses, a sub-editor from a popular science magazine discovered that a story he'd brought for examination by the rest of the group fell apart when the story's convoluted and vague words were translated into simple, specific ones. It became clear that an expert science writer had little idea of the logic of the story he'd filed for editing. Complicated words turned the logic of an apparently world-changing product breakthrough into nonsense.

The sub-editor went pale and excused himself to call his office. He'd brought a live story to the course and it needed further editing before being published. Oops.

No matter how expert you are in a niche subject, and even if you write for similar experts, it makes sense to write as simply as possible. Even if fellow experts understand your jargon, simple words push you towards greater clarity of thought and your writing will hit home faster, carrying greater impact.

Read your work aloud and you'll quickly spot words and phrases that beg to be simplified. If you wouldn't use a word in speech, change it. It's a sign that you're trying to impress, or write in a way you think is expected, rather than in a way that's direct, straightforward and authentic.

Simplicity transmits meaning quickly. Anything else earmarks you as a timewaster.

'The road to hell is paved with adverbs.'

STEPHEN KING

FAQs

Isn't this pandering to the lowest common denominator?

Definitely not. It sounds as if you want to train your readers to struggle through the kind of language they don't need to read. Are you indulging in some misdirection at your readers' expense? Are you trying to show off or intimidate others? Let your knowledge and insights show your business smarts without disguising what you know with jargon and pompous words.

What if people expect complicated language?

Expecting it doesn't mean they want it. Your readers may even work in an *Emperor's New Clothes* culture, one where everyone secretly wants to say the obvious — that jargon and pompous language get in the way of success — but no one wants to be the first to say it. Everyone yearns for writing that's quick to read, and easy to understand. When someone delivers simple, concrete writing that's clear and tight, what do you think your readers' reactions will be? Glass of champagne? Promotion? Bonus?

I'm beginning to worry that my writing is going to stand out like a sore thumb. Why me?

Why not? Standing out is what you want, isn't it? Someone has to show the way and, since you're reading this book, you've opted to become that person. How can you nudge the world if no one's recognising you as someone with a distinctive view and an authentic way of expressing it? Go for it.

'The most valuable of all talents is that of never using two words where one will do.'

THOMAS JEFFERSON

CHAPTER TWELVE

To make a long story short... cut it

WORDS don't die if you cut them. Neither do they sulk and refuse to be used in the future. If you can cut words without losing meaning, you should. When you ditch the fat, writing gains power.

Tabloid newspapers and short blogs seem livelier than those we call the quality press partly for this reason. Tabloids use shorter words, and they use fewer of them. It generally works.

Any first draft can be cut sensibly without being damaged. Learn from the best: Stephen King knows he writes long and chooses — without reading a word — to cut 20 per cent of his first drafts.

It sounds arbitrary, and it is. But it's based on the idea that we can always find something that serves no purpose. If you have followed the process, you should have less attachment to your words since you'll be more concerned about writing concisely and clearly.

Cut to the bone and readers will peg you as a clear thinker who gets quickly to the point.

Don't try to sweat over possible cuts on your first draft. If you practise using the process well, your first drafts will steadily improve. Cuts can easily be made during editing and rewriting.

You may find it useful to make an educated decision about how long you want your document to be, and then aim to make your words fit. This isn't the tail wagging the dog if you choose a reasonable length; it's a discipline that works well within sensible boundaries. You need to respect readers' time. Choosing to work within limits often encourages creativity.

Since you are building on advice from previous chapters you will already have taken steps towards constructing sentences that are direct and straightforward. You now want to cut words, phrases and entire sentences where they aren't needed.

Here are some common phrases ripe for culling.

We ought to stress that...

When you want to make a point, be definite, using strong words. Dilute it with this kind of weak phrasing, and your message loses its emphasis.

It is only fair to point out that...

This sounds defensive, as if you're trying to avoid being fair. If you really want to be fair, write it clearly.

I would like to take the opportunity to thank you for...

This doesn't thank anyone. It acknowledges the chance to do it — without expressing any thanks. When you want to show gratitude in writing, don't forget to do it.

We are sorry you feel we have given bad service on this occasion...

This is a non-apology, passing the buck back to the complainant. If you want to apologise, do it. If you don't see the need for an apology, say nothing. Readers loathe this kind of non-apology. It feels as if you'd rather people kept complaints to themselves.

Let's look at some before-and-after examples from a local government letter about a disputed penalty charge notice — a car parking ticket to you and me.

I am in receipt of your correspondence regarding the above Penalty Charge Notice. You were parked in a Pay & Display bay without clearly displaying a valid Pay & Display ticket.

I note your comments in your most recent communication. And thank you for providing a photocopy of your Pay & Display ticket. However, the photocopy you have provided is of too poor quality to make a decision to cancel or waive your Penalty Charge Notice. Please provide a legible copy of your Pay & Display ticket

in the next 14 days and your case may be reviewed.

However, if you wish to contest the matter further you should await the issue of the 'Notice to Owner'. The Notice to Owner will be sent to the registered keeper of the vehicle after 28 days has [sic] elapsed from the date of issue of the Penalty Charge Notice if the Notice remains unpaid.

This version of the letter has 148 words, and 25 per cent passive sentences. It is pompous, evasive and confusing.

I have your recent letter about the above Penalty Charge Notice. Thank you for your further comments and the photocopy of your Pay & Display ticket.

However, you parked in a Pay & Display bay without (clearly) displaying a valid ticket. The photocopy you sent is of too poor quality for me to decide to cancel or waive the Notice. Send a legible image in the next 14 days and I may review your case.

Otherwise, if you want to continue your challenge, please wait until we issue the Notice to Owner. We will send this to the vehicle's registered keeper if the Penalty Charge Notice remains unpaid 28 days after the date of issue.

This version is shorter at 113 words, and more direct with no passive sentences. It feels friendlier, despite the continuing resistance to the ticket appeal, and offers clear instructions. It's not going to thrill the reader, but that's not the fault of the language.

Sometimes we find simple cuts. On other occasions, we need to redraft rambling sentences where redundancy is hidden. On rare occasions, we'll realise the need for more extensive restructuring, perhaps of an entire section.

This calls for a forensic approach to writing. What do individual words and phrases mean? What do they add? Do you need them? What impression does the writing make? Will it win readers and achieve your goals? Is there anything you needn't say?

If you want to nudge the world, you don't need lots of words, just smart ones.

'I try to leave out the parts that people skip.'

ELMORE LEONARD

FAQs

Is there such a thing as writing that's too short?
Not if it's written well.

Are you sure?
Yes.

So why do I have the feeling that I need to write more?
You probably realise that you haven't written something well enough. Perhaps you tried to fix this by trying to express it differently in a new phrase, sentence or paragraph. Then you kept both versions, because neither really worked. Cut them and start again. Concentrate on getting a clear message across, saying it well and without using unnecessary words. Say it once, and then stop. With practice, you'll develop an instinct that tells you when you're done.

Can I cut too much?
Only if you are unclear about what you're trying to say and lose the sense of what's important. When you know your purpose, your readers' needs and have clear knowledge and insights to share, you're unlikely to cut vital information.

People commonly tell me they haven't the space to include everything they need to use. When they discover how to cut the fat, they find they have enough room to say everything they want — and they deliver more value in fewer words.

If I do this, will my writing feel abrupt?
Good writing never feels abrupt. It feels concise.

'Pithy sentences are like sharp nails driving truth into our memories.'

DIDEROT

CHAPTER THIRTEEN
Don't bury the lead

BEGIN each paragraph with powerful statements that get straight to the point and you give readers a reason to stick with you. Start by writing about the last thing that anyone wants or needs to know, and you're in trouble.

Following a Cabinet meeting held at 10 Downing Street this morning, the Chancellor of the Exchequer announced plans to abolish income tax.

Which part of this sentence holds the most interest? The abolition of income tax or the preamble about the Cabinet meeting? No contest. There are two clauses and we're starting with the least interesting one. Yet business writers fall easily into this writing trap and wonder why their work doesn't... work.

Fortunately, this is an easy fix. Swap the clauses and the sentence reads like this...

Plans to abolish income tax were announced today by the Chancellor of the Exchequer, following a Cabinet meeting held at 10 Downing Street this morning.

Of course, you may feel the details about the Cabinet meeting to be irrelevant at this point in your document, and context will help you to decide if you're right. If you decide they are, feel free to cut that clause. Business documents often include information at inappropriate points purely because the writer is afraid of short sentences.

Yet there's nothing wrong with short sentences. An ideal sentence length is around 15-20 words, but some will have as few as three; maybe fewer... And some will be whoppers, with good reason. Short sentences offer you the freedom to have longer than average ones that fully explain a point at greater length.

We want variety and flow. Monotony gets in the way of reading. We notice a tedious pattern to the writing instead of taking in the message. Rhythm in our choice of sentence structure helps to keep us reading, as we anticipate the useful nuggets that will come next.

For these reasons, we won't want to ditch all sentences that start with a preamble clause. Writing becomes structurally repetitive if you do and you will have fallen into a writing-by-numbers approach.

My tip is to open paragraphs with a strong sentence that instantly carries your most interesting information. Save the softer version, leading with a subsidiary clause, for the end of some of your paragraphs. Doing this will stop your paragraphs from petering away...

But you're still not writing a mystery novel. Your readers' time is hard won and precious. Show them respect and don't hang around. They'll reward you by reading on.

THE SHORT SENTENCE AVOIDANCE PERIL

Trying to avoid short sentences opens a further trap that can turn writing to mush.

If you're interested in tomorrow's weather, forecasters predict heavy snowfall for most of the country.

Snow falls whether you're interested in it or not. Ignoring the weather won't stop you from being snowed in. The phrase *If you're interested...* lengthens the sentence while avoiding starting with a direct statement about key information — and it tells your readers that you don't understand your own writing.

We're here to help you to expand your business, which makes our latest offer really exciting.

Readers will resist the logical nonsense of this sentence, even if they don't fully understand why the words prompt them to recoil. Instinctively they know this writing is not to be trusted. Someone wanting to help a business to expand is great. It doesn't make the latest offer more exciting than it already is.

Readers have instincts too.

'...when writing, always hook the reader with your first sentence.'

SPIDER ROBINSON

FAQs

If subsidiary clauses are bad, why do I need them at all?
Sentences that start with a subsidiary clause have a structure that delays the main point. They aren't automatically bad. It's just that they often feel... flat. If you try to hit a top note with every sentence, you will exhaust your readers. But you may want to ration sentences that start with the least interesting information. My advice is to use them at the end of some, although not all, paragraphs. But don't take this as a rule. We want tips and guidelines, not rules.

There's a time and place for all style choices. When you know why certain ways of writing create specific impressions in your readers, you can work on creating the impression you want through the way you write.

Ultimately, what you write and how you write is a reflection of you. You want to feel comfortable with what you send out.

So as long as I'm upfront most of the time, I can save something until the end?

Er... is this a trick question? There's a difference between moving information from your first sentence to the final page — and structuring sentences for variety. Avoid obsessing about the need for a 'wow' finish for your document. If you've followed the process, you'll have said more than enough to impress your readers without sweating over a phoney end.

How will I know if my direct approach is working?

If you tell a joke and people laugh, the joke's funny and you've delivered it well. If you hold your readers' attention to the end of your documents, your writing approach is working on at least one level. But using the process is the real key to writing well. Clear thinking leads to clear writing.

Sounds great. Is that it?

Are you joking? First drafts are just the beginning. Read on...

'That isn't writing at all, it's typing.'

TRUMAN CAPOTE

CHAPTER FOURTEEN
Now for the real work

FIRST drafts are a start, but you're far from finished. The act of writing is not only about committing your thoughts and ideas to paper; it's also about finding what they are — as you write. So if the penny drops about your real message as you type the final word, don't beat yourself up.

We're used to reading polished work in newspapers, magazines, books, business blogs, reports and marketing material. Little, if any, of it is first-draft writing. Sensible writers put their work through an editing wringer, inviting someone to find flaws and identify areas for improvement.

Journalists have sub-editors; book writers have editors too. None of these writers have the time to put their work in a drawer, returning to it when they have regained enough objectivity to assess it realistically. The world is moving too fast for that luxury. And there's no point deluding ourselves that we can be objective about our writing as we finish our first draft. If we thought our writing was flawed, we'd have written it differently.

Practical reasons also force revisions onto writing that's already well crafted. Lack of space in a newspaper or magazine forces cuts that make writers and sub-editors weep at the loss of good material. Web writing has restrictions in different ways, prompted by the need to stop people from clicking to another site. Books may need to be culled to a length that suits their market niche.

You probably don't have a skilled editor to hand. What you need is objective help from well-chosen helpers who are armed with a tight brief on what you want from them. But, you have further work to do before asking for feedback.

If you had any *Eureka!* moments while writing — and made notes on them — deal with these now. It also makes sense to read your document thoroughly and make notes of areas you already feel need revision.

Read a paper version of your work, even if your intention is to send a digital version to readers. The mere act of reading a hard copy changes perspective; you will spot flaws you might otherwise miss.

Ask yourself some process-led questions as you read.

- Does your writing serve your purpose — for you and your readers? Does it fall short? What can you do to fix it or make it more powerful?

- Do any of your *Eureka!* moments create structural issues? Are they an easy drop-in? Or do they demand research?

- How might readers respond to your work? Is that what you want?

- Are there obvious gaps? Can you fix them now?

- Does your structure work? Does it need tweaking? Or major surgery? Or no work at all?

- Is the language tight or flabby? Direct or evasive? Clear or muddled? Too loud or too soft?

You will naturally have greater objectivity on the early parts of the process, purely because you tackled these first. The last thing you did — committing your ideas to words — is where you will see the fewest flaws.

You want your document in the best shape possible when it goes to your helpers. They aren't expert editors, remember. Avoid expecting them to do all the diagnostic work. Fix the obvious flaws, particularly where changes are short and easy to do. Make notes for areas that need considerable work or where you want feedback.

All of this work still counts as your first draft.

ASK FOR HELP, BUT PICK THE RIGHT PEOPLE

People love to give feedback. It makes them feel valued — up to the point where you ignore every comment they make. At this point, they will feel you've wasted their time and, in future, may resist pleas for help.

Caving in —adopting any and all suggestions, no matter how much you disagree with them — is counterproductive and damaging. So choose your helpers well, and brief them wisely, if you want to avoid this kind of awkward situation.

You're on a path to more authentic writing and it's scary. What you need at this point may not be what you want. You'll be tempted to look for kindness and smiles of reassurance. Don't. You need the truth you're aiming to deliver to your readers.

But you're not after sadistic shredding of your work either. You want balance and reason, not extremes. So choose a mix of helpers. How many you recruit is up to you.

Look for someone who's good at strategic thinking and seeing the big picture. They're likely to spot flaws in your purpose and structure and raise unanswered questions readers are likely to ask.

Find someone who's good at detail and has a solid grasp of the language, someone who hates jargon and who will spot research gaps. Be warned: arguments over commas may arise.

If you want feedback on a sensitive email, a quick reaction from one person is all you'll need.

The bigger the document, the longer it takes to read and absorb, and the harder it becomes to spot flaws that are more than simple typos and language glitches. You want to be thorough, but keep the numbers down. You're not recruiting a football team.

For particularly crucial documents, where you have more than one helper, adopt a sensible system.

- Circulate one document within the group. Give four people the same document to read at the same time and you'll get back four separate, and probably conflicting, sets of comments.

- Ask helpers to comment on a paper version of your document. People will be drawn to rewriting if you give them a digital one; rewriting is your task, not theirs.

- It helps to ask people to read with specific tasks in mind — it helps them to focus. Try to stick to this order — purpose and readership, consistency of information, structure, spelling and language.

THE BRIEF WAY TO GOOD FEEDBACK

YOUR feedback team doesn't automatically know what you want your writing to achieve or who you're aiming to reach. You hope it's obvious, but if your writing has strayed, they may guess incorrectly.

An invitation to *'Let me know what you think of this'* is no briefing at all. It's a veiled request for people to love your writing and tell you it's brilliant. You may get an unpleasant surprise, when people give you a blow-by-blow plan for how they would rewrite it — if only they could be bothered.

If you want useful feedback, give a clear brief with details about what you want people to consider, and — equally important — what you want them to ignore.

Tell your helpers the goal of your writing and who it's aimed at — in reasonable detail. If your helpers are similar to your readers, tell them. Likewise, tell them if your readers are the opposite.

Ask your helpers if they feel you've left out vital information. It's easy to become so expert that you forget others know less than you. Chances are, you'll have what you need at your fingertips and can easily drop it in.

If you've deviated from common templates or norms in favour of a more creative structure of your own, well done! Don't forget to tell your helpers why you've made this choice, and ask if they feel it works. Do this in all areas where you're trying to take a fresh approach. Your helpers aren't necessarily trying to nudge the world. You are. Helpers may need to hear your rationale for being different.

Likewise, if you have no-go areas you've been forced to adopt, tell your helpers. Brief comments are fine. But you don't want to waste time with overly detailed suggestions on areas you can't change.

If you already have instincts that tell you where you have work to do, tip off your helpers and ask for their take. You may be overanxious, or your instincts may be spot on.

It may sound as if you're trying to justify your writing in advance of anyone reading it. Make it clear that you're not. Explain that it's important to avoid treating feedback as a game of *'if they don't spot something, it can't be wrong'*. This is not how feedback works. You want constructive criticism. But you don't have professional editors, so give as much genuine guidance as you can.

Stress the need for truthful comment, not reassurance and kindness, and promise to accept criticism with grace. Invite suggestions for problem areas — if your helpers have ideas of their own. Hearing criticism without also hearing proposals for improvement is often frustrating. Be kind. Bear in mind that helpers aren't always right — and they're approaching your writing with a fresh eye and less time to come up with answers than you've had.

Some areas demand special attention and are worth particular mention.

Factual errors and possible misinterpretation
Factual errors, no matter how minor, may turn your work into a pack of cards that collapses because it lacks foundation. Factual mistakes undermine your credibility too.

Ever read a news story about your own

industry or personal obsession, and spotted an error or misinterpretation? How did you view the rest of the story, and other stories from the same newspaper or website? Mistrust would be my guess. *If they can get this one thing wrong, what else did they get wrong in areas where I'm no expert and won't see a mistake?*

While writing this book, I spotted an error in a non-fiction book which referred to *Dr No* as the film featuring James Bond strapped to a metal block with a high-powered laser heading towards his genitals. It's *Goldfinger*, not *Dr No*. It's a tiny slip in a book that isn't even about film. But my faith in the writer was temporarily damaged. No errors are too small to be insignificant.

Credibility can disappear in a moment, and take years to earn back; the accuracy of your thoughts forms the basis of your writing. Your ideal fact checker is a scientist. If you don't know one, go for an anal person who gives great attention to detail and who has no yearning to please you.

You will slip up, so invite vigorous challenge, especially if you are your company's expert in a particular area. When proven wrong, experts are doubly embarrassed.

Cross-check information that should agree. These may be at opposite ends of your document and be hard to spot. And remember that information may seem credible and still be wrong, while outrageous facts may be accurate.

Accuracy slips are a nightmare you want to

discover long before you've pinged your writing into the world to be greeted with scorn and laughter, and a new career that involves little writing.

Likely reader reaction

Some people have a stronger sense of empathy than others. Recruit them: you want someone who can sit comfortably in your readers' shoes and judge the likely reaction to your writing. These are people who would queue up to be part of Michael Corleone's organised massacre in *The Godfather*, happy to align themselves with the devil to protect the family. They'd be equally happy to eat the mean-spirited psychiatrist at the end of *Silence of the Lambs* because they're cheering for Hannibal Lecter to get out his knife and fork. They have no qualms in cheering for the baddy — they have a strong sense of empathy. Your readers should be a piece of cake for them.

Bear in mind that reader reaction is not about instantly selling someone on your ideas. It's about engagement, dialogue and possibilities. Silence is your enemy. You need reaction if you are to stand out and serve your readers. And ruffling feathers may be the best result in some circumstances.

You probably know someone who takes the opposite stance in any conversation — just for the hell of it. Ask this person to give you reader reaction feedback, but bear in mind that you believe in what you're saying, while they are aiming for effect.

You want to anticipate all likely responses, even those that annoy you greatly... Deal with these now. Whatever you do, don't hide tricky areas. Bring them out and plant a flag on them. Turn them to your advantage. Tackle this part of feedback well and you'll send out the vibe of being someone who thinks of everything and isn't afraid to tackle tough questions.

Language feedback

Our use of language is a mix of cut-and-dried precision and subjective style. It's also about *you*, *your* readers and *your* aim to nudge the world with writing that shows you at your best.

This is the area where you are likely to feel most insecure. Listen to your helpers but allow instinct to guide you too. Your helpers will sometimes be wrong. If you aren't sure that suggestions will improve your work, ignore them or rewrite sentences, taking a route you know is correct or accepted usage.

Embrace corrections you know to be no-brainers. Pick and choose from the subjective ones. Ask yourself how strongly your readers are likely to feel about strict grammar rules. Will they accept a more casual style? Is that choice appropriate and an accurate reflection of you?

With a mix of views, and your own instincts, you'll find the right tone and style for your purpose.

WHAT COULD POSSIBLY GO WRONG?

No matter how well you choose your helpers, and no matter how well you brief them, issues will crop up.

- People will be kind, tell you that your writing works well, and you'll feel a 'but' hanging in the air. Push. You are waiting for the penny to drop. And there's usually a penny.

  Your helpers have their own internal database, but their archiving is no better than yours. Without good reason to make a comment, they may leave the 'but...' unanswered. It doesn't mean there isn't a problem. If they can't explain, work out the issue yourself.

- People will over-edit and suggest a rewrite in the style they'd use — if they were the writer.

  You may have been soft with your brief or they're trying to show off, or indulging in a power trip. Or it may be all three. Cherry pick from their suggestions and do your own thing.

- People will suggest a placc where they believe a problem exists, but it feels wrong.

  Your helpers are probably right and wrong at the same time. There is a problem, but it's not where they think it is. They may see a research gap when the problem is structure. They may see a language flaw when the issue is one of reader engagement. Sometimes you need to be a detective to pin down the problem.

- People will spot a flaw — and it makes you incandescent with rage.

  Sadly, they're right; you need to drop any resistance. Your anger is for one of three reasons.

  One, you have a gap in your research. You started writing with a nagging thought that something was missing, but you ignored it. You hit the gap and wrote around it because you didn't want to interrupt your flow. You reread your work and ignored the doubt that resurfaced. You deluded yourself that no one would notice. And someone did...

  Two, someone has spotted some weak information, something you fixated on including, purely because it was a nightmare to discover. The only person who could divulge it had to be tracked across three continents, several time zones, and you had to sweet-talk your way past two assistants determined to block you. You thought you were going to discover something fascinating; instead, you were given something useless. Cut it.

Third, you're being precious about your words. Toughen up. Everything can be improved. Bestselling and award winning writers accept criticism. Why not you? Writing is personal, even in business, but you don't have to take feedback as an attack. If someone doesn't care for your writing, it doesn't mean they hate you. It means they want better and think you capable of producing it.

WHAT ELSE CAN I DO?

When you have tons of feedback, and are making sensible revisions, you still have tactics that can produce useful pointers.

- **Read your work aloud**

  Do this somewhere private to avoid annoying colleagues. Writers are often advised to write as they speak; the aim is to use words you use when speaking, as long as you avoid slang or made-up words from the 'hood. Reading words aloud helps you to pick up stray ones that sound pompous and stand out from your simple, direct work.

  If you stumble through sentences while reading aloud, your readers will stumble in their heads. If you wince, it's a clue there's something to change. If you pause, it's a clue... if anything prompts you to stop reading, it's an alarm bell.

■ Check more than spelling

While you are checking spelling, check that word's meaning too. Sometimes you'll find you need a different word.

■ Make it look good

Tight, insightful copy that's a joy to read may benefit from visual pyrotechnics that add to the strong impression you want to make. But this introduces new pitfalls.

Use a reasonable size and style of font across a width that's easy to follow. Any text with more than 75 characters on one line is hard to read for anything longer than a caption. Our eyes have to move as we read and that makes reading slow.

Beware of running text across lush, complex visuals. Make sure that the text you've carefully crafted is readable.

Double check any text that has passed through the hands of a graphic designer, even if you made no corrections to it. You won't know if they've experimented with the layout and then had to retype your text. Check everything.

■ Find one final helper

When you've finished revisions, you'll want a fresh pair of eyes able to spot final flaws. Your initial group of helpers will have lost their objectivity and they'll see what they expect to see.

Change words at the beginning of your document and you may have missed something that needs changing at the end. Change numbers in your text, and they may contradict a chart or table. This kind of cross-referencing is easy to get wrong, allowing inconsistency to creep in. It damages your credibility by introducing errors that aren't a mistake in your thinking or research.

A final pass at your writing should be simple proofreading, but ask for the same rigour you expected of your original group of helpers and then decide if suggestions are fixing a problem or just changing your work. Your final helper may spot a major error yet mistrust their judgment in the misguided belief that others would already have spotted it. Press them to speak up if they feel something is a major speed bump.

At the same time, don't feel obliged to reinvent the wheel; you'll never reach perfection. Trying to get there runs the risk of overcooking your work.

In small offices, a fresh pair of eyes at this stage can be a rarity. For one-man businesses, it's non-existent. Leave your work overnight if you can, read it after a good night's sleep and then send it out. Or team up with another one-man band and act as a mutual safety net.

WHAT NEXT?

When you've sent your writing out into the world, try not to sweat over how it will be received. You've done your utmost to make it fresh and authentic, with some depth to your insights and suggestions. But it's undeniably scary when you're trying to take a new approach.

You've taken some important steps to add good writing to your working toolbox and your skill will improve with steady practice. Use the process regularly and your confidence will grow. The payoff for your work is huge.

You will never lose your fear of failing. No writer does. But you can put it in its rightful place — in the background, urging you to do well.

Each piece of writing is a fresh mission and offers you the challenge of stamping your fingerprint on it. Treat each blank page or screen as a chance to nudge the world a little, and you'll get to your seat at the cool kids' table where the important decisions are made.

'If you show someone something you've written, you give them a sharpened stake, lie down in your coffin, and say: "When you're ready".'

DAVID MITCHELL

FAQs

If I have a lot of rewriting to do, doesn't that mean I've failed?

No. You're not perfect. You will slip up with your first draft. Writing isn't just a way of expressing what you've already worked out. It's also a discovering process, finding out what you think and feel — as you write. It's entirely natural that work needs revision.

What if I disagree with people who give me feedback?

It's your choice. If you have a good reason to ignore suggestions, ignore them. But don't resist arbitrarily. People are trying to help.

Isn't it just a lot of extra work?

Not always. A lot of feedback will be a checking and challenging process, aiming at making sure you are factually correct and saying exactly what you mean in as few words as possible.

Will I get fewer comments as my writing improves?

You probably will. But sometimes you will write

yourself into a mess for reasons related only to a particular project. If that happens, don't beat yourself up. Make the process a habit and you'll gain confidence and skill. Go and nudge the world.

GETTING TO THE FINISH

Do you have a proven system for feedback and editing?

_____

_____

_____

_____

Do you give colleagues a precise brief?

_____

_____

_____

_____

Do you know when to stop rewriting?

_____

_____

_____

_____

'My attitude towards punctuation is that it ought to be as conventional as possible. The game of golf would lose a great deal if croquet mallets and billiard cues were allowed on the putting green. You ought to be able to show that you can do it a good deal better than anyone else with the regular tools before you have a license to bring in your own improvements.'

ERNEST HEMINGWAY

CHAPTER FIFTEEN
Know your shit, or know you're shit

PUNCTUATION is the written equivalent of the body language and tone of voice we use when having a face to face conversation. You pause, make a hand gesture, raise your voice or lower it. These visual tics show people how to interpret the nuances of what you mean.

Punctuation serves the same purpose in writing. It helps you to say more, say it more interestingly and get your meaning across to readers at first reading.

The web is full of fun examples that bring out the clear need for punctuation.

Let's eat grandma!

Let's eat, grandma!

I like cooking my family and my pets.

I like cooking, my family and my pets.

Some examples aren't even about food.

A woman, without her man, is nothing.

A woman: without her, man is nothing.

Mother to be attacked on waste land.

Mother-to-be attacked on waste land.

She was sick and tired of watching TV.

She was sick, and tired of watching TV.

The underlying purpose of punctuation is to show readers how words and strings of words are related, separated and emphasised. It's about communication, not passing exams.

Several comprehensive books about punctuation are available online and in bookshops. My aim with this brief guide is to give you the absolute essentials you need to know to survive your working day.

APOSTROPHES

The most common grammar mistake, according to website spellchecker.net, is a misplaced or missing apostrophe. The easiest way to check if you are using an apostrophe correctly is to ask if you're cutting letters, numbers, or words. If you are, you're probably right.

Let's get the biggest offender out of the way.

It's only ever means **it is or it has**.
Anything else is **its**.

It's a lovely day...

British history has <u>its</u> equivalent in the Magna Carta.

You have no excuse for getting this wrong again. *EVER*.

Take a similar approach with other word contractions. Think of where the letters or numbers are missing and use it as a guide to where to place an apostrophe.

<u>She'll</u> instead of <u>she will.</u>

The <u>'30s</u> instead of the <u>1930s</u>.
NEVER the **30's**.

Use apostrophes where you want to show that something belongs to someone, allowing you to cut words.

The man's wig *(the wig belonging to the man)* **was eaten by the family's dog** *(the dog belonging to the family).*

Several neighbours' houses *(the houses belonging to the neighbours)* **were burgled.**

I sent you Mr Jones's business plan.

Or...

I sent you Mr Jones' business plan.

Pedants will rage about whether or not to use **s's** in the Mr Jones example. My general advice is to choose — and stick with your decision.

Sarah's roast potatoes were better than the chef's.

In this final example, you don't need to repeat the reference to *roast potatoes* — you're already implying that the chef has some too.

Avoid the greengrocers' apostrophe trap. You shop for *potatoes*, not *potato's* or *potatoe's*. You buy *books* and *bags*, not *book's* and *bag's*.

There are exceptions where apostrophes are used in the plurals of a handful of random, mostly short words — *do's* and *don'ts*, *P's* and *Q's*.

One final warning: avoid wrapping them around words, using them as single quotation marks, to show where you are uncertain of the meaning or want to show a slight difference in 'meaning'. This is far from a safe approach.

You may get sued on the grounds that the apostrophes imply the opposite meaning.

'Lady' may be interpreted as **prostitute**.

'Gentleman' may be taken to mean **crook**.

'Authentic' may be read as **phoney**.

BRACKETS

Wrap these around a string of optional words, ones that could easily be cut from a sentence without losing the nub of a statement.

We use brackets (even when they contain useless information, and even when we're using ones we should call parentheses) because we prefer them to commas.

This example shows the main issue. Brackets usually give a signal that they contain something we probably don't want or need to know. Avoid using them — where you can.

COLONS

Colons have three main uses:
To start a vertical list — as I've shown above — or a running text list.

She has several great qualities: charm, intelligence and lots of money.

To act as a drum roll or punch line, taking us from the start of an idea to its conclusion.

Jim only has one issue: his entire personality.

To introduce quoted speech.

Sue said: 'Learn how to use punctuation well.'

COMMAS

Single commas separate two parts of a sentence.

Although hard hats were widely available, most workmen weren't wearing one.

He's a great leader, but not very charismatic.

A pair of commas cordons off information that is an aside — just like brackets [ ] and parentheses ( ). Beware: you need to know what information is an aside, and what is essential to the meaning.

The passengers who wore seatbelts were unhurt.

Without commas around *who wore seatbelts* the sentence means only those passengers who buckled up were unhurt. The rest probably ended up in hospital.

The passengers, who wore seatbelts, were unhurt.

All of these passengers were unhurt. They happened to have buckled up, information that has been used purely as description — thanks to the use of two commas.

And commas are helpful in lists.

I need to shop for tea, bread, milk and wine.

Now, we were all told at school never to use a comma before the final item in a list — as shown above. But that doesn't take into account the Oxford comma, an optional one traditionally used by printers, readers and editors at Oxford University Press. It's also known as the serial comma.

Why do we need it? Well, the point is to avoid ambiguity. Look at these examples:

This week's interviews include Susan Feehan, a fitness fanatic and the UK's worst cook.

Now, I don't mind people being misled about me being a fitness fanatic when I'm not. But I don't care to be labelled as the UK's worst cook as I'm fairly useful with a spatula.

This week's interviews include Susan Feehan, a fitness fanatic, and the UK's worst cook.

This version gets me off the hook for being a dreadful cook, even if the fitness fanatic label lingers.

Academic authorities divide sharply into *for* and *against* factions, the against lobby claiming that losing it saves space. Seriously? One tiny comma? Until someone forces a referendum to settle the issue — use it or lose it, depending on possible ambiguity. Be prepared for arguments.

Best practice is to use commas sparingly. If your sentence seems cluttered with them, don't just leave them out. Try making your sentence simpler so you need fewer of them.

DASHES

You may want to use dashes instead of a pair of commas to mark an aside, particularly if you need extra visual clues on how to read a sentence.

> **Their new house — in a leafy London suburb, I believe — cost more than £2m.**

Or you may want to use a dash to show an afterthought — unless you feel they look ugly.

EXCLAMATION MARKS

These are commonly, and badly, used in an attempt to prompt you to feel amazed! Or to make you laugh! Using an exclamation mark usually signals that you're not being amazing or funny at all!!!

Under no circumstances do you need more than one. Even if you have to yell: 'FIRE!' Confine their use to social media — if you must — or for true exclamations, such as when you need to escape disaster or certain death.

HYPHENS

Hyphens create links between individual words you want to be read as one unit, mostly to form a compound adjective. We refer to *computer-based work*, *short-term goals*, and *out-of-school activity*.

You may see words used with and without hyphens, each version being correct. The key is to decide if two or more words are being used to describe something or someone. If they are, join them with hyphens

The chancellor will discuss the <u>balance of payments</u> with the media.

The chancellor will discuss the <u>balance-of-payments</u> problem with the media.

In the second version, *balance of payments* is being used purely to describe a problem, not as a noun in its own right.

Watch out for phrases that change from a phrasal verb (a main verb plus an adverb or preposition) to a noun. We use hyphens when using a phrasal verb as a noun.

We decided to <u>stop off</u> at the motorway services on our way home. *(phrasal verb)*

We knew there would be a <u>stop-off</u> at the motorway services on our way home. *(phrasal noun)*

When we bring new words into the language, we often use hyphens until they become familiar and normal enough to become a single word — *E-mail* turning into *email*.

Fractions and numbers from 21 to 99 are usually hyphenated when written as words. *One-third, twenty-one,* and *ninety-nine.* Watch out for where context changes the meaning...

250-odd people — means roughly 250 people.

250 odd people — means 250 strange people.

When in doubt, check with your dictionary or your office style guide. Style guide? You don't have one? Check out the useful books reference list...

SEMICOLONS

These often seem to be the deepest, darkest puzzle in punctuation; you may never have been tempted to use one. The good thing is they aren't compulsory, so you've never been wrong.

If you want to join two related sentences together — use a semicolon. You may find semicolons useful if you're wary of using short sentences.

Thanks for replying to our Christmas office party invitation; it's a shame you won't be able to come.

It's that simple. Mostly...

Of course, you may need them in a complex list to show where items are grouped and separated.

The UK's fastest-growing industries are: shipbuilding; agriculture and livestock; retail, clothing and crafts; car manufacture; and financial services.

The semicolons show separate industry sectors, while the commas show smaller divisions within them.

Soak up these punctuation basics; they're as much as you're likely to need for most of your working day.

You can also download a free pocket punctuation crib from my website and leave it on your desktop for quick reference. You'll find it, and other free tools, at www.susanfeehan.com.

'The most essential gift for a good writer is a built-in, shock-proof shit detector.'

ERNEST HEMINGWAY

'If you have any young friends who aspire to become writers, the second greatest favour you can do them is to present them with copies of **The Elements of Style***. The first greatest, of course, is to shoot them now, while they're happy.'*

DOROTHY PARKER

CHAPTER SIXTEEN
Books that make you look really smart

WRITING well demands precision as well as the ability to take a broad view. The forensic part of writing comes more easily with time and practice, but you will always need good reference books, no matter how much your confidence grows. An experienced car mechanic has access to specification documents and standard operating manuals for each marque and model, particularly since manufacturers add new features regularly.

Words, and our language skills, aren't set in stone either. Anyone who writes needs the writing equivalent of car manuals and you need to keep them up to date. Mastery of the language isn't always about what you know. It's about knowing where to find answers when you're stuck. Looking something up is never a sign of weakness.

This book list is based on finding quick answers that fill an instant need. None of these books is about exploring the roots of words going back to olde English or other languages. Neither do they try to turn you into an academic. Pick and choose which ones suit you best.

I'd suggest buying the paperback versions on the grounds that reference ebooks sound like a good idea, but are often harder to use when you want to flick through for a quick fix.

You can always keep yourself on track to better writing with the resources available at my blog and website.

www.susanfeehan.com

'Any word you have to hunt for in a thesaurus is the wrong word. There are no exceptions to this rule.'

STEPHEN KING

FIVE-STAR ESSENTIALS

The Elements of Style by Struck & White

This is a tiny book, and a bit stern. You may find the grammar terminology a little alien, but stick with it. This book is packed with useful tips and considered a standard work. The bonus of its being short means you'll spend less time looking things up, while getting a lot of bang for your buck.

Troublesome Words by Bill Bryson

This delivers exactly what the title promises, and sorts out the dilemmas of the most troublesome words in alphabetical order — a great idea. If you are puzzled by the difference between *affect* and *effect*, then this is the book for you. It rates four+ stars on Amazon with good reason. Bryson uses examples from national newspapers and you may find it reassuring to discover how seasoned pros get things wrong.

The Economist Style Guide

Every business or organisation needs its own style guide and you have to start somewhere. Do you refer to companies as singular or plural? Do you put a full stop after Dr or Mr? Where do you use abbreviations, italics and capital letters? A style guide should save you from taking decisions about these and other general issues with each piece of writing. Life is too short to argue with your colleagues about minutiae that don't need daily rehashing, particularly when you want to nudge the world into being a better place.

You might choose an alternative guide based on *The Guardian's* or *The Daily Telegraph's* usage. It's your call — but convince everyone you work with to stick to the same choice or arguments will continue.

New Oxford Dictionary for Writers and Editors by Oxford University Press.

This is more than an average dictionary, although it's still alphabetical. It contains a host of what might seem like random information, but it's packed with stuff you will want to know at some time or another in your writing life.

For instance, on the first page of the As, you will discover the exact size of A3 paper, that Abba has two meanings other than a Swedish pop group, and that aardwolf is a real African mammal of the hyena family. What's not to like? You may even win back the cost of buying the book in pub quizzes.

An up-to-date dictionary — hard copy or digital version

Online dictionaries contradict my harder-to-use argument — but make sure your colleagues use the same brand or you'll argue over differences; refer back to my 'life is too short' point. The issue is not whether Collins is better than Oxford, it's about consistency. Buy one. Use it.

You need a dictionary that's up to date: no more than two years old, please. If you have a hard-copy dictionary that Noah brought out of the Ark, throw it away or use it as a coffee coaster. Noah didn't have a clue about *twerking* or *selfies* — but they're in the dictionary.

Who Touched Base in My Thought Shower?: A Treasury of Unbearable Office Jargon by Steven Poole

If office jargon like *blue-sky thinking* and *low-hanging fruit* makes you gag — and it should — buy this and spread the word. This will make you laugh and, hopefully, start an underground cell to undermine this kind of abuse.

What? No thesaurus?

If you don't already know a word without tracking it down via a thesaurus, you shouldn't use it. Bestselling author Stephen King is against the thesaurus, and I agree. Stick with words you know. Use the devil's instrument and you'll be tempted to use a long, pompous word you've just discovered purely to impress someone. That's plain wrong. Expand your vocabulary by reading, not by cheating.

'The only thing you absolutely have to know is the location of the library.'

ALBERT EINSTEIN

FOUR-STAR GOODIES

If you suddenly decide to join the grammar police and want to go further into the nuances of language craft skills, you may want to invest in some of the following books. There's no obligation to do so; feel free to stop at the five-star essentials.

Oxford Guide to Plain English by Martin Cutts

This is a solid book covering all kinds of writing, with sections as varied as *Writing short sentences and clear paragraphs, Pitching your writing at the right level,* and *Clarity for the Web.* You may want to skip over the section at the beginning on why Plain English is needed and how it has developed around the world.

The Ladybird Book of Spelling and Grammar

This is no joke. The Ladybird book is a great one that writers in the know recommend to adults and children alike. The book is out of print, but versions are sometimes available on Amazon as trade ins at varied prices. If you have a small relative with one of these, 'borrow' it.

The Complete Plain Words by Sir Ernest Gowers

The Penguin Dictionary of English Grammar by RL Trask

The Penguin Guide to Punctuation by RL Trask

This is a handy trio for those who become anal about their language usage. They are available on Amazon and in good bookshops.

Eats, shoots and leaves: The Zero Tolerance Approach to Punctuation by Lynne Truss

This will make you laugh, and maybe fear for your life at the hands of language pedants. Expect a fun read more than a reference book.

My Grammar and I (Or Should That Be Me?): Old-School Ways to Sharpen Your English by Caroline Taggart and JA Wines.

This does for grammar what *Eats, shoots and leaves* does for punctuation, which is to make it fun. If you went to the dentist on the day they taught grammar at your school, this may be for you.

'Good English, well spoken and well written, will open more doors than a college degree. Bad English will slam doors you didn't even know existed.'

WILLIAM RASPBERRY

'If you can't annoy somebody, there is little point in writing.'

KINGSLEY AMIS

CHAPTER SEVENTEEN

An A-Z of writing tips to give you a taste for precision.

 **is for – affect**

AFFECT as a verb means to influence — *driving while drunk can affect your insurance* — or to pretend to have or feel something — *he affected a love of European cinema.*

It's a weak verb, one that may leave us guessing about meaning. *None of us will be affected by the company's reorganisation.* Is this a good or bad thing? Would we be in line for a promotion or pay rise? Or might we be tossed onto the street with a pitiful pay off?

Use a stronger verb.

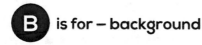 **is for – background**

SOMETIMES we face the dilemma of how to handle background when we write to experts.

We don't want to preach to the choir, but we want to show that we've done our homework. The answer is to slip in useful background as an aside.

The closure of a third of the bank's branches, *driven by the trebling of internet banking during the past five years*, will be complete within three months.

 **is for – can**

CAN shows what you are capable of doing, *may* shows whether you have permission to do it. If you had a weak bladder at school, and asked: *'Can I go to the toilet?'* your teacher may already have pointed out the difference. Teachers can be annoying...

C is also for — confusable words

SOME words seem so alike — in sound or spelling—that we mix their meanings. *Continual* refers to something that repeatedly happens. *Continuous* means it carries on without a break.

 **is for – destroy**

DESTROY is a completed word that needs no further hype. If we write that a city was *completely destroyed*, we're over-egging our work. However, we may write that it was *partly destroyed*, because it's hard to describe it any other way.

We also return from work and declare ourselves to be *half-dead*, although I doubt we expect to be taken seriously. Neither does any woman claim to be *mostly pregnant*.

is for – estimated

ESTIMATED does not need added qualification. *The profits have been estimated at about £60million.* Cut *about*.

is for – fact

WE can usually change the phrases *despite the fact that* or *due to the fact that* to *although* or *because* — and lose nothing.

Profits went up, *despite the fact that* turnover went down, *due to the fact that* departments became more efficient.

Profits went up, *although* turnover went down, *because* departments became more efficient.

We don't need *true facts* either. If they're not true, they're rumours, theories or propaganda.

F is also for — fragments

FOR a sentence to be complete, you need to have a subject and a verb. *I prefer short meetings.* Anything else is a fragment. *Boring meeting.* No grammar checking software likes fragments.

You may decide to keep them, particularly when you don't mind being informal and when you're sure readers won't object. *I went to the conference. Pretty awesome.* Use them when they serve a point or help to establish a particular tone. No point being a rebel for the hell of it.

G is for – growth

GROWTH seems an innocuous word, but we often forget that it involves... growth. If we want to imply shrinkage, decline, or even running on the spot, then we need a different word. Our sales *growth* has *halted/stalled/fallen back* in the past year. Wrong.

H is for – habit

HABITS are regular. Don't say *usual habit*. Or *customary* or *regular*. Just habit... unless it's new, then use *new*.

I is for – if and when

MAKE up your mind. Choose one. *If we...* or *when we...* not *if and when we.*

 **is for – join**

JOIN does not need to be followed by *together*. *These two people are joined together in marriage...* Not needed.

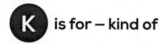 **is for – kind of**

WE say: *This is the kind of sentence we want to read.* Or *These are the kinds of sentences we want to read.* This kind of writing shows consistency in using singular/plural.

L **is for – lay/lie**

BOY does this pairing cause trouble... first let's nail the definition of each verb. *Lay* means to put something or someone down. *Susan laid down the gun. Lie* means to rest or recline. *Susan's sofa is covered with hair because Scout, her cat, often lies there.*

To *lay* can become *lay(s), laid* and *laying* as your tense changes. *To lie* becomes *lie(s), lay, lain* and *lying*. The simple past tense of *lie* is the same as the simple present tense of *lay. Susan's sofa was covered with hair because Scout, her cat, often lay there.* No wonder we get confused.

 **is for – major**

AN overused word. *Major medical breakthrough. Major budget increase.* Major adds nothing. Aim for detail that defines how major something is. How many lives will a medical advance save? How much is the budget increase?

While we're here, we can usually change *majority* to *most*. And we never need *the vast majority of...* How vast is it?

 is for – near disaster

ANOTHER word pairing that often produces nonsense. *Susan swerved her car and avoided a near disaster with the lorry.* No, Susan had a near disaster. Swerving saved her from a disaster.

 is for – oxymoron

A PHRASE where two apparently contradictory meanings come together and still make sense to us. *Clearly misunderstood* is one of them, so is *organised mess* and *only choice*. Be careful. Look hard and you'll find we don't need them.

 is for – paragraph

BRING related points together, using paragraphs as your unit of thought. When you start a new paragraph, you should be shifting your focus to a new topic, or a sub-division of your existing one.

Q is for – quotation marks

DECIDE a style for quotes from speeches, reports and other instances where you want to use someone else's wording. *'Use single quote marks and then "doubles" where you "quote" within a quote,' said Susan. "Or go 'crazy' and do the opposite," she said.* Use a colon to introduce speech. *Susan said: 'What has the cat done with my wine?'*

R is for – revert

DON'T use *revert back*. Or *cut back*. *We revert to a previous plan. We learn of budget cuts.* We don't need more.

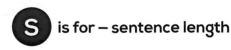

S is for – sentence length

THE longer sentences are, the harder they are to read. Short is good. Look at any sentences above 30 words and try to chop them up, eliminate redundancy or rephrase them in a simpler form. If all else fails, start again.

T is for – their/there/they're

THEIR = possessive. *It was their car.*

THERE = location. *Their car was parked over there.*

THEY'RE = they are. *They're driving away in their car.*

U is for – unique

UNIQUE means one of a kind. It doesn't mean amazing, brilliant or just a great product or offer.

V is for – very

VERY is overused and often props up a weak word. When you are tempted to use it, try to use a stronger expression. Find further detail if you need to. *Very large. Very good.* Neither is *very* helpful.

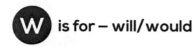

W is for – will/would

THE issue between *will* and *would* is clarity. It's the difference between knowing that something *may* happen and knowing that it *will*. *The office refurbishment would cost £2million* implies you need approval of the budget and the go-ahead to make the refurb happen. *The office refurbishment will cost £2million* says that it is going ahead with an agreed budget. Don't be wishy-washy where you can be definite, and avoid taking a step too far when you have doubt.

X is for – Xmas

PLEASE don't; it's a cheap way to shorten the word. It's Christmas.

Y is for – years' time

YEAR is a time period. Don't double up.

Z is for – zealot

BECOME one of these: a person who is uncompromising in the pursuit of their ideals.

ABOUT THE AUTHOR

SUSAN FEEHAN has a lifelong passion for words — as a journalist, a university lecturer in journalism, a business writing mentor, and a screenwriter.

Susan has zig-zagged through the business-to-business, consumer and customer publishing sectors, working her way up to editor. She has trained sub-editors for major UK magazine publishers, and helped multinational companies, along with professional and public bodies, to transform their approach to writing.

Susan lectured in journalism at City University and the University of the Arts in London. At UAL, Susan mentored students through 'journalism boot camp' — the weekly production of a 32-page newspaper for a 25,000 plus strong student readership.

Ideas generated by Susan's sub-editing experiences drove her to screenwriting. Of the five feature scripts Susan has written, two have won writing awards. Most are either 'in development' or are at the fundraising stage; one is on its way to becoming a comic novel.

Susan stays sane by helping business people to write well.

www.susanfeehan.com